QUEBEC

QUEBEC
The Challenge of Independence

Anne Griffin

RUTHERFORD • MADISON • TEANECK
FAIRLEIGH DICKINSON UNIVERSITY PRESS
LONDON AND TORONTO: ASSOCIATED UNIVERSITY PRESSES

Associated University Presses
440 Forsgate Drive
Cranbury, NJ 08512

Associated University Presses
25 Sicilian Avenue
London WC1A 2QH, England

Associated University Presses
2133 Royal Windsor Drive
Unit 1
Mississauga, Ontario
Canada L5J 1K5

Library of Congress Cataloging in Publication Data

Griffin, Anne, 1940–
    Quebec, the challenge of independence.

    Bibliography: p.
    Includes index.
    1. Québec (Province)—History—Autonomy and
independence movements.   2. Québec (Province)—Politics
and government—1960–   . I. Title.
F1053.2.G74   1983   971.4'04   81-72054
ISBN 0-8386-3135-5

Printed in the United States of America

Contents

Preface

On November 15, 1976, the people of Quebec voted into power the Parti Québécois, a political party committed to the independence of Quebec and to eventual separation from Canada. The Parti Québécois was a minority government: although it held a majority of seats in Quebec's legislature, the National Assembly, it had been elected by only 41.4 percent of the votes cast. Yet to many observers, the event was as baffling as it was unexpected: Why would Quebecers—even a minority of them—wish to renounce their ties with Canada, after nearly two decades of political and economic integration, in favor of a much less certain future as an independent state? Objectively, independence appeared to make little sense: by separating, Quebecers would forfeit many of the gains they had worked hardest to achieve. Others regarded the election as a type of brinkmanship, a ploy in Quebec's continuing campaign for increased autonomy within the Canadian federation. Still others dismissed the results of the election as a mere wish for a new administration. But for all of them, the old question has taken on a new urgency: "What does Quebec want?"

This study of the Separatist movement in Quebec is an attempt to understand a political and social phenomenon that is becoming increasingly significant in this last third of the twentieth century. Scarcely a week goes by that we are not reminded, sometimes by eloquent appeal, but more often by violent deeds or bloody confrontation, of some nation's demand for independence. Separatist movements may erupt in areas which have appeared stable for decades and even centuries, but frequently they are the result of an ongoing tension between an ethnic group and the sovereign state in which it is incorporated. Quebec, Brittany, Scotland, Wales, Northern Ireland, the Kurds and the Basques have figured prominently in the news of recent months.

Why do separatist movements arise? It is relatively easy to list their general preconditions. It is more difficult, though, to tell which of these factors are salient. Even with specific cases, it is often hard to identify the point at which the movement began and to determine what, precisely, precipitated it. Geographical isolation, the absence of jurisdictional fragmentation, persistent ethnic and cultural identities embodied in race, language and religion, memories of conquest or colonization, the impact of modernization and the altered perceptions it arouses, the sense of economic deprivation, the loss of faith in the legitimacy of the central government, and the absence of suitable institutions for the redress of political grievances have all been identified as preconditions of Separatism.[1]

There is, in addition, the impact of historical events. The breakup of Europe's colonial empires in the period after 1950 set a momentum which continues to this day. For centuries, conquered territories had broken off from various empires and successfully established themselves as sovereign states. But many of these "new" territories had at one time existed as sovereign states and thus enjoyed the tradition, if not the recent experience, of self-government; furthermore, the European examples, at least—Norway, Ireland, Hungary, or Czechoslovakia—were generally regarded as developed countries. By contrast, the African nations which became independent after 1960 were not only traditional societies with little experience in national administration but states whose boundaries had been arbitrarily defined, a century earlier, by competition among colonial powers. The achievement of independence, first by Algeria and later by her sub-Saharan neighbors, discredited the old arguments that a sufficient level of political and economic development had to be reached before independence could be granted. It is interesting that in Quebec the resurgence of Separatism coincided with the loss of France's colonial empire and de Gaulle's rise to power in the 1950s. A "Why not here?" attitude may be detected in the period after 1958.

Another important feature in the development of separatist movements is leadership. It is the leader who gives focus to the social or political movement, whose pronouncements can be identified as its "official" position. Leaders often guide social movements from their earliest stages, but they can also appear at a later phase. René Lévesque, for example, did not become active in Quebec's independence movement until 1967, ten years after its founding.

Yet in the final analysis we must consider, as does John R. Wood, "whether . . . *psychological preconditions* are what galvanize all other preconditions of secession." Beneath the "objective" arguments for independence "there remains the emotional element of the desire for an independent homeland on the part of the secessionists [and the] desire to preserve the union on the part of loyalists to the larger state." At a deeper level, it is possible to discern an appeal not only to identifiable goals such as home rule but to individual needs, both conscious and unconscious, for power, physical amenities, self-respect, ideological direction, and the like. Specific motives of this nature may be observed in the case of Quebec, but it is important to emphasize that the overall implications of psychological motives are cross-cultural.

This case study examines a phenomenon that has obvious parallels with other separatist movements. Some basic questions are raised. If Separatism has its roots in a minority "consciousness," what causes it to overrun the limits of mere consciousness and emerge as a political movement? How does it increase and sustain its appeal? And finally, what are the implications of Separatism for the survival of bi- and multi-ethnic states?

Quebec Separatism sustains itself by satisfying the perceived needs of certain individuals, needs which have been defined by the circumstances of Quebec's history. Although it is questionable whether Separatism appeals to more than a minority of the population, it provides a set of values around which those who adhere to it can structure or restructure their lives. At present, the independence movement in Quebec appears capable of increasing its appeal to the extent that it can convince more French Canadians that these values will satisfy their overall needs.

Separatism functions not only because it offers the individual a given amount of these values, but because of the specific way in which these values interact. This process of interaction is referred to here as facilitation; it is the basis of the entire substructure which reinforces the rational elements of political choice. The patterns of facilitation tend to reflect the traditional values of French Canadian society and are an important factor in the success of the independence movement.

The research for this study began with a series of interviews conducted in New York, Montreal, Quebec City, and in rural areas of Quebec. The richness of the material gained in these interviews made a series of case studies virtually imperative; these are presented in part 2. The tabulable results of the interviews are presented in part 3. These two sections are intended as complementary; the subjective impressions recorded in part 2 are supported by the analytical material in part 3. Part 1 offers an explanation of the social, historical, and psychological factors that have contributed to the emergence of Separatism in Quebec. Finally, part 4 considers the implications of Quebec's experience for other bi- and multi-ethnic states.

From its inception this study has benefited frm the counsel and encouragement of friends, colleagues, and teachers, I would like to thank Alfred de Grazia, whose suggestion of the hexagonal paradigms used to record patterns of facilitation in part 3 is gratefully acknowledged, and also Anthony Astrachan, Terry N. Clark, André Dupuis, Germaine Ellis, Gisbert H. Flanz, Claude Frenette, Thaddeus R. Gatza, Jacques Jolicoeur, Norbert Lascoste, Ruth S. Mechaneck, Francisco José Moreno, Claude Morin, Maurice Pinard, the late Guy Poliquin, H. Mark Roelofs, Maurice Sauvé, the late Ernest Schachtel, Howard L. Singer, and Eric Valentine. Finally, to Jay Lefer, who has provided moral and physical support for so many years, and to our sons, David and Teddy, I owe a very special debt.

NOTES

1. For a comprehensive summary of the literature on Separatism, see John R. Wood, "Secession: A Comparative Analytical Framework," *Canadian Journal of Political Science* 14: 107–34 (1981).

2. Ibid., p. 120.

Introduction by Andrew M. Greeley

After reading Anne Griffin's fascinating manuscript, I found myself wondering not why Canada is threatened with dissolution but why the Canadian experiment has lasted so long. Quebecers are a conquered people captured by English tyranny about the same time my ancestors in Ireland were definitively brought under the English yoke. They were granted, much earlier than the Irish, internal political rights of their own, though they continued to be victims of economic injustice. The Canadian experiment has made major efforts to facilitate the indentification of Quebecers with the heritage of the Canadian nation, including granting them access to the prime ministership. Ironically indeed, English Canadians have probably done more than any other majority of people in the world to facilitate the integration into their nation of the minority cultures and peoples—everything, it sometimes seems to me when I read English Canadians or hear them talk. They are trying to understand the Canada problem from the viewpoint of the Quebecers (just as the French Canadians are quite incapable of understanding the viewpoint of so-called new Canadians—cultural pluralism for ourselves, but not for you latecomers!). Yet for all the faith in rationalism, liberal democracy, and scientific progress that mark the naïve Lockeian era that came to an end in Vietnam or at Hiroshima or in August 1914 (take your pick), cultural residues die hard. The memories of past injustices are not easily put aside, especially when present injustice and insensitivity keep fanning the flame. The nineteenth-century nation states of Europe are, to a greater or lesser extent, torn by resurgent separatism; the Basques, the Flemings, the Tyroleans, the Catalonians, the Welsh, the Bretons, and above all the Irish, are not content with the arrangements that mark the Victorian Era. There is no reason to think that Quebecers would remain indefinitely content with such arrangements either.

To the outsider, Quebec separatism seems "irrational" in the same sense that the behavior of the Irish Republican Army seems irrational. Quebec probably is not viable as a totally separate nation. In terms of economic, financial, and industrial growth, the continuation of the present arrangement makes sense. A Canadian civil war is "unthinkable." Why risk peace and prosperity because of ancient wrongs? Why dredge up the memories of the past conflicts and thus endanger present tranquility?

Such surely is the view of many English Canadians and also of many sympathetic but confused outsiders (and many American Irish befuddled by the conflict in the land of their ancestors).

The issue is our "model" of human nature. If the human species was made up of, let us say, archangels, or some other totally rational and hence totally calculating creatures, then ethnicity would not be reviving. If we were the rootless, heritageless universalists of whom Professor Orlando Patterson is so fond, then we would not value the cultures we inherit. We would not be offended by historic injustices. We would not seek to keep alive our tradition. We would, in other words, be content to let the winners of the past conflicts continue to be the winners.

Yet such a model of human nature is extraordinarily naïve, as Professor Griffin's book makes abundantly clear. We are richer, more complex, more intricate, more vengeful, and more loyal than Professor Patterson's disembodied universalism would have us believe. It may be that we all *ought* to be universalists. It may be that Quebecers, the Irish, and all other inheritors of a "lost" cause should abandon their past memories in the interest of logical, rational universalism. It is not, however, likely that they will, or even that they can, and that if one is to benefit from the integrative and universalistic dimensions of cultural heritages, then one must also put up with the angry, bitter, and devisive memories. It will do no good at all to tell those who value their cultural heritages that they are being irrational. It will not help the delicate negotiations which may preoccupy Canada for years to tell Quebecers that their behavior is not rational. Instead, it would be helpful to try to understand the problem from the point of view of Quebec. Professor Griffin's book is an extremely helpful exercise in searching for that understanding.

The non-Canadian can at least express the hope that the two parties to the great Canadian debate may be able to work out a compromise that will satisfy a decisive majority of French Canadians and at the same time maintain some sort of national unity. One cannot say that the Canadian attempt at federalism has failed.

The question, rather, is whether that experiment is flexible enough to be able to absorb the sorts of dynamics which Professor Griffin describes. The outsider can only hope that the Canadian experiment will continue to be successful for finally the solutions to the problems of cultural pluralism are to be found in toleration, compromise, and pluralistic immigration rather than the tearing apart of the fragile cords that bind human beings together in organized political structures.

QUEBEC

Part 1
The Situation Stated

1 • The Ideology of Survival

A white cross on an azure field, a white fleur-de-lys in each quadrant, the banner of Quebec flies over the National Assembly in Quebec City and over countless gas stations in the Laurentians. A nation remembers. These colors, once carried by a regiment of Louis XV, testify to the French fact in North America and to the persistence of a memory that has made possible the survival of a nation.[1]

The ideology of survival, as expressed in the motto *Exister c'est survivre* ("to exist is to survive") has characterized Quebec's history and her relations with Canada for over 200 years, and it has left a distinct impression on the lives of her people. It has persisted because of the blend of memory and amnesia, myth and politics which has attended the needs of Quebecers—needs defined by the prevailing power structure, social, economic and geographic conditions, and above all by the role of the Roman Catholic Church. So enduring was the influence of this institution in prescribing those values which came to dominate life in Quebec that even its marasmus in recent years has left them more or less intact. Every pastor kept in his repertory images of a legendary past, of a society consecrated to the glory of God. These he recalled for his parishoners as the proud treasury of a communal heritage. At the opposite end of their common existence lay the promise of an even greater splendor. In between stretched the dreariness of their daily life, more drab for some than for others, but seen by all as a time of trial, or at best of preparation. Those who remembered would keep the faith, never losing sight of their final reward.

To survive was to bear witness to a past that might otherwise be extinguished. It meant to get along, to continue to exist in the face of all obstacles. To be sure, survival has been a central theme in the Canadian experience. Geography and climate, relations with the Indians, political and social diversities within her borders and the development of a powerful neighbor to the south have posed a continuing challenge. The survival of a Canadian nation is premised at least in part on the reconciliation of these diversities and the accommodation of particular interests to the needs of the whole.[2] A very different attitude has existed among Quebecers. Here, the concept of nation was equated with the specific culture, language, and religion by which they identified themselves. National survival has meant, at the very least, the survival of these specific forms. Consciously or unconsciously, the ideology of survival has been the motive force in Quebec's subsequent political history. Humiliations have been suffered and accommodations made in order that a nation might continue.

When a nation's survival is at stake, memory becomes supremely important. Memory is essential both as a principle for action and as a rationale for survival itself. A nation remembers in order to survive, but at the same time it survives in order to remember. In such circumstances, the institutions that guard and define it rise to positions of dominance. Thus the role of the Church in both Quebec and Ireland, and the significance of the Bible among the Jews of the Diaspora, and the charismatic appeal of leaders capable of finding in the past lessons to be applied in the present and future. In Quebec events have traditionally been measured against an epic past which ended abruptly with General Montcalm's defeat on the Plains of Abraham and five years of military rule. Canon Lionel Groulx, Quebec's intellectual leader in the first half of this century, made frequent reference to *"Notre maître le passé"* ("Our master, the past"), establishing it as a guiding principle for social and political action.[3]

As a symbol of identification, memory is also an instrument of survival. More compellingly even than language, memory defines membership in a group and is a mark of belonging. To proclaim, "I remember," as do all license plates now issued in Quebec, is to identify common past experience as the basis of present values and community. Those who share a common memory are related in a way that those who do not can never be. They will persist together for as long as they can communicate this shared memory with one another. People who remember the same things (or claim to or wish to) will also tend to understand current conditions in similar ways.

A nation that has a memory has a distinct identity, a particular vision of itself. To remember the Plains of Abraham means to have some specific feelings about the position of Quebec in the Canadian confederation. To remember that Canada was French before it was English means to treasure what is French about Canada, to want to speak French, the language of one's forebears, not English, the language of the conqueror. To remember Papineau and the failure of his rebellion meant, until recently, to abandon all hope of independence. It meant to forget about the success of the American Revolution and other movements of independence. Memory, in the service of survival, is highly selective.

Consciously, then, memory serves as a powerful symbol of belonging and as a means of recording and explaining past experiences. It shapes one's understanding of the past and the lessons to be learned from it. But memory is also latent in countless ordinary acts and in the way they are experienced. Keeping faith with the past involves more than recording it. Through tradition, values, and attitudes toward life's events, memory is kept alive even when the origins of such responses are forgotten. Unconsciously, people preserve their own history. Conditions may change, but values tend to endure, even over long periods of time and through widespread social and political change. What develops into a way of life is not easily abandoned, even in the face of changing circumstances. Time has translated the need to survive as Frenchmen into a need to survive as Quebecers. But the fact remains that even after a period of unparalleled social and economic integration, assimilation is anathema.

There has been a vast difference between those values operative in Quebec and those adhered to elsewhere in Canada. The dominance of the Church and her role as power broker in relations with the English and later with Anglo-Canadians tended to depoliticize life among most Quebecers. As a result, they have been much less concerned with politics than their Anglo-Saxon counterparts. Similarly, the emphasis on spiritual rather than material values, coupled with an unfavorable economic structure, meant that Quebecers traditionally have been less concerned with wealth and its accumulation. An individual's worth, in his own eyes and those of his peers, was calculated not in terms of power or wealth—these had already been preempted—but respect and learning. Although power and wealth might be courted with little chance of success, respect and learning were more readily accessible to those who sought them. These were promised in full measure to the deserving.

These realities have changed somewhat in recent years, but certain consistencies remain. Quebecers, as a rule, still emphasize the cognitive values—not only formal education and other forms of acquired knowledge but comprehensive explanation and understanding of their place in history, in the international community, and with Canada. Saint John the Baptist, Quebec's patron and protector since colonial times, was described by a young priest in curiously secular terms: "a colossus who sees the whole world, who knows where he is going." The role of the seer, capable of predicting and even prescribing future events in the light of past experience has undergone a similar process. The decline in religious faith has been accompanied by an enlargement of the role of secular institutions and the assumption by political parties of many functions traditionally the task of the Church. The ideology of survival has been secularized but it remains intact.

The symbols of national survival have changed, too. Traditionally, survival was equated with retaining such things as language and religion, together with a sense of uniqueness and moral worth. The twin forces of increased contact with Anglo-Canadians and secularization have expanded the meaning of survival, so that many Quebecers now perceive it in economic and political terms as well. On a personal level, wealth and power may continue to be relatively unimportant. But at the communal level, an increasing number now understand survival in terms also of economic viability and political autonomy. Many Quebecers have no difficulty in reconciling these goals with Canadian federalism. They tend to support Canada's policy of biculturalism and bilingualism; they are able to tolerate the inevitable inequities of a bicultural society. But for a large and growing minority there is only one option: to support the independence of Quebec.

This book is about these people. It is also about independence and the steps, long and sure or short and tentative, that some of them have taken in that direction. It explains why *they* want independence, and how their lives have changed as a result. On the surface it would seem that the main thing most of them have in common is an attitude about the Parti Québécois: that it represents, at the very least, a viable option for the future of Quebec. On closer observation it becomes apparent that their actual attitudes toward independence vary almost as broadly as their individual experience. At the deepest level they share a set of historical conditions and present circumstances to which they respond. Although certain culturally specific ways of responding can perhaps be identified, each person can be said to have arrived individually at his determination. In 1973, when the interviews on which this book is based were conducted, the Parti Québécois did not yet have broad popular support. Most people were unwilling to admit publicly that they supported the independence movement. Joining the party was, for most of them, a step taken in resistance to social pressure, not in response to it.

This book also attempts to explain the appeal of a movement in its earliest phase, that is, during the period when it appeals to only a minority and is generally regarded as having little chance of success. What must it offer if it is to become a full-fledged social movement? What gives it that cutting edge that enables it to rip through men's apathy and resistance to change? Which realities give it force and sustain it through that period of vital growth while it gains political significance? Which evoke the needed response?

The compelling quality of the present movement in Quebec can best be understood in terms of three basic factors and the way in which they interrelate. These can be identified as *historical circumstance*, *present relevance* and *personal response*.

Historical circumstance consists of history that is experienced directly, remembered consciously, or recorded unconsciously. It may in some cases involve events that never occurred, or that took place in a manner very different from the way in which they were recorded. This does not matter. What does matter is that these events took place under circumstances that caused them to be recorded as they were, and that they are remembered as such.

Historical circumstances define communities. Quebecers—just as Irish, Basques, Ibos, Bengalis, or black Americans—experience certain inherited conditions, political, social, and economic, that outsiders do not. In addition, each community has certain common ways of remembering not shared by others. For such groups, historical events are not easily undone.

But in order to be believable and thus to be of service to the present, history must undergo a continuous process of editing and reassessment. The psychoanalyst Ernest Schachtel, in his essay on memory and childhood amnesia, argues that it is the present person who remembers, who sorts out and reassesses past events in the light of present needs, interests, insecurities, and ambitions.[4] In a community undergoing significant social change, the individual who is able to undertake this function for the group by presenting a clear and compelling paradigm, credible because it contains elements which are both reassuringly familiar and predictive of the future, will rise to a position of dominance. Historically, and throughout much of the world even today, religious institutions have filled this role. They have done so because religion's two main functions have traditionally been, as Andrew M. Greeley points out, interpretive and communal.⁵ But whether religious or secular, institutions succeed when they are capable of providing a set of values around which individuals are able to structure or restructure their lives. The success of the independence movement in Quebec, especially since the advent of René Lévesque and the founding of the Parti Québécois, can be attributed in large measure to the skill with which it addresses itself to the historically conditioned needs of Quebecers.

History, of course, is not everything. To succeed, a movement must have *current relevance:* it must appeal to present needs in order to evoke a response which is politically significant. There are essentially two kinds of needs, those things people value and are likely to want as a result of historical conditions, and those they are likely to want as a result of current conditions. But in many cases these needs are the same. People's responses to current crises are conditioned by past experience. In Germany, Hitler successfully manipulated a centuries-old tradition of anti-Semitism during the period of widespread economic dislocation which followed defeat in World War I. In France, General de Gaulle returned to power proclaiming, "I am the Jeanne d'Arc of Modern France." In Iran, the long tradition of Islam and distrust of modernization gave vital support to the people's resistance to a despotic Shah. In Quebec the Parti Québécois has based its appeal on two long-cherished ideals, autonomy and survival. However, the view that these goals could be secured only through political and economic independence did not even begin to attain political viability until the late 1950s, when political and economic integration had begun to threaten Quebec's identity and sense of uniqueness. Then the issue of political independence became significant, in the sense that large numbers of people were willing to consider it as an option for the future of Quebec. In each of these cases, political movements became relevant when they addressed present crises in terms acceptable to a substantial number of people.

So it is the individual who must ultimately be the judge of whether a policy or "option," as Lévesque calls it, is acceptable. It is the individual who responds to an incipient independence movement, accepting its principles as valid and adjusting his behavior and attitudes to this new perception of reality. To evoke this *individual response*, an ideology must give hope that it will satisfy those needs which are most important in his life and that it can do so in a way that no competing ideology can.

What are needs? Most basically, needs are values which serve as standards for human attitudes and behavior. They are perceived as needs when people feel they ought to have them. For example, when Jean Dupont, a garage mechanic, says that the present economic structure is draining Quebec, he is recognizing wealth as a value toward which political change might be directed. In criticizing the present system and implying that economic well-being is both desirable and something Quebecers ought to work toward, he is identifying wealth as a general or societal need, though not one he necessarily shares. But if he expresses the view that he personally should have more spending power than he now has, he is indicating that he too has a need for this particular value.

All people are attracted to institutions and ideologies that emphasize the particular values they have come to deem important. They tend to view political movements that emphasize these values as most likely to satisfy their needs and those of their community. What is not generally recognized is that for most people, the values expressed by the movement exert a far greater appeal than do its professed goals. Thus, a growing number of Quebecers believe in independence not because they have always regarded it as the only way to resolve the question of their status as a people, to gain a sense of national identity, or to prosper economically, but because the Parti Québécois, the chief institution of this movement, makes such a strong appeal to these values. Others, rejecting independence as an ultimate goal, vote P.Q. because they are generally sympathetic with its ideals. No competing political or social movement has been able to focus its appeal so successfully. Joining an ideological movement can also bring about a rash of secondary advantages, realized over time, as a result of participating. These gains are rarely apparent to the individual at the time of joining. Yet they are often an essential factor in maintaining the loyalty of a movement's adherents and in assuring its ultimate success.

Those who supported independence realized these gains in two ways. There was, first, the satisfaction achieved in joining the movement, and second, the satisfaction gained from belonging. For in committing oneself to an ideological movement two significant phases are involved. The first, which many of us have experienced at one time or another, is the "moment of recognition." This is usually preceded by "revelation," acceptance of the new paradigm, and of the ideals and goals of the movement. It is an initial reconciliation of the conflict between individual values and external reality, or, more precisely, the choice of new values that will reflect a new construction of that reality. The second, and the most important in maintaining the momentum of any movement, is sustained "involvement." What keeps a person involved after he or she has accepted the essential "truth" of an ideology? What insulates him from the counterarguments of competing ideologies? If supporting the Parti Québécois has already satisfied a person's long-standing need to understand his status in Quebec and in history (and whatever else might have been anticipated as a result), what keeps him from retreating to the security of a more traditional party, one which does not seek any significant structural change in the society but instead tries to reconcile similar reforms with an existing structure?

The hypothesis offered here is that, over time, participating in an ideological movement may satisfy certain preexisting needs. These needs, defined by historical and current conditions, are satisfied in two main ways: *initially*, with the intellectual recognition that "there are others whose goals and values are not only something like my own, but who have thought carefully about where we're going, and are right," and *over time*, through the secondary advantages which come as a consequence of participating. Often these advantages have little to do with joining a movement and accepting its ideology; they are rather a "payoff" for sustained involvement and commitment. In some cases a movement can focus its secondary appeal so successfully that it becomes the chief means for satisfying those individual needs that have come to predominate in a particular society or culture. Such movements are likely to be enormously successful. No two people respond in exactly the same way, but certain patterns and configurations tend to repeat themselves within a given setting. Thus certain political movements will evoke a broad response in certain cultures and virtually none in others. A similarity of needs—or at least of perceived needs—is basic to mass appeal. A movement will gain or lose strength as it is able to retain the loyalty of its adherents by satisfying these long-standing needs.

To survive and prosper, an ideological movement must appeal at both levels. Initially, its professed goals must correspond with the hopes, dreams, fears, and sense of self of the people it claims to represent. Not all of these attitudes need be conscious ones, but there must be at least an element of conscious recognition that the movement "speaks for me" or "expresses something I feel strongly about." Over time, a movement must also deliver sufficient satisfaction to keep such people involved. These advantages can be obvious, as when a person who has experienced increasing frustrations as a member of the Liberal party quits and subsequently stands for election as a Péquiste. But usually they are subtle. After spending most of his adult life in the United States and the Bahamas, Jean Dupont feels "at home" in Quebec for the first time in his life. A college professor enjoys his friends more, now that they have a common commitment. A businessman claims to have more respect for his Anglo-Saxon colleagues. Sebastian Dupré, the young priest, "sees where he is going."

Thus the phenomenal success of the independence movement in Quebec. Its main appeal is twofold, based on its offerings of ideological leadership and community. It emerged at a time when the institutions which traditionally had filled these roles were weakening—the Church, through urbanization and secularization, and the Union Nationale, the conservative, nationalist political party, through internal corruption and political defeat. By identifying itself as a vessel of national survival and the sole interpreter of Quebec's past, present, and future and by recalling them to participation in a new, secular and national community, the Parti Québécois has assumed, for an increasing number of people, a position of dominance paralleled only by the traditional leadership of the Church.

In a now-classical work on the nature of mass movements, Eric Hoffer argued persuasively that all ideological movements exert a similar appeal, and that people are distinguished not by the character of their individual beliefs but by the intensity with which they adhere to them. "When people are ripe for a mass movement, they are ususally ripe for any effective movement, and not solely for one with a particular doctrine or purpose." All mass movements are competitive and therefore interchangeable. The partisan of one is also a prime target for its competitor.[6]

The case studies presented here offer a different argument. There are, it is true, distinct personality differences among the subjects, and those who were most committed to the movement tended to resemble each other more than those who were less involved. Persons for whom the cognitive values—memory, learning, general knowledge, and understanding—were most important tended to be more heavily committed to social change than to others, and to this extent, Hoffer's analysis holds. But Hoffer's thesis fails precisely because it is too broad. In attempting to explain the "true believer," that extreme type of individual who is drawn to any mass ideology, he overlooks the problem of those who are attracted to some and not to others. He fails to distinguish between the broad-scale mass movement and the nationally and culturally specific one. In focusing only on the person who believes, and not on what he believes in, he neglects an issue of primary importance: the compelling quality of the movements themselves.

Few, if any, of the people described in this book could be called true believers. Most of them would be quite capable of living with no strong commitment or formal belief system, though less happily. For them, the appeal of the independence movement lies in its reconstructive quality. In each case, there is an empirical correspondence between the internal reality of the individual—his memory, hopes, needs, and fears—and the external reality of the movement. By skillfully framing its rationale and structure to correspond with these internal realities, the leaders of the independence movement have been able to focus its appeal in terms of the needs, both conscious and unconscious, of an increasing number of Quebecers. Its compelling nature can be understood, and its success predicted, in terms of the extent to which these two realities correspond.

The following chapters will show how a specific movement becomes an integral part of people's lives. To do this, it will be necessary to identify a set of broadly defined values and to describe the specific appeals of Quebec's independence movement as variants of these. There have been a number of attempts to develop such a scheme; the one used here is essentially Lasswell's,[7] as adapted by de Grazia. Power, Wealth, Respect (including self-respect), Enlightenment, Affection, and Health and Well-being are identified as six basic values; they also represent categories of need as well as gain.[8] According to Lasswell and Kaplan, "In some form and to some degree, these values . . . always play a role." But, they caution, these values are understood differently by each culture and even by each individual. "What values are operative and to what extent can be understood only by specific inquiry." Chapters 2 and 3 therefore attempt to outline the historical conditions and present state of the independence movement in Quebec; part 2, through a series of case studies, shows how for certain people the movement provides the most definitive answer to the question of survival and to their individual needs, thus evoking a favorable personal response.

Several concepts have been used repeatedly in the present chapter, among them nation, memory, ideology, and movement. Because these ideas recur fairly frequently in this book and support much of its argument, and because each has been defined elsewhere in a number of ways, it seems appropriate to define them as they are used here.

A *nation* is a community which comes into being when a people identifies itself in terms of a distinct history and a common commit-ment to the future. Race, blood, geographical boundaries, lan-guage, and religion may reinforce this relatedness, as in Quebec, but no one of these factors is essential. Since the sixteenth century, nations increasingly have been constituted as states, with the result that now statehood is broadly considered to be the final stage in the development of a nation, but some nations have existed for cen-turies without such a formal apparatus of their own. The difficulty arises with the perception that the state which claims political au-thority over the community is not its legitimate representative. In Quebec, the memory of the conquest serves to reinforce this at-titude; similar perceptions seem to accompany most movements of independence and national liberation.

Memory is the capacity to record, organize, recall, and under-stand events. Memory and experience interact: memory conditions reactions to present situations, but at the same time it is continually edited and reevaluated in the light of contemporary conditions and experience. Memory is both individual and collective. While it is the individual who remembers, and while his own experience is more acutely perceived, he nevertheless participates, through in-teraction with others, in a shared consciousness. At the collective level, memory can be understood as the net sum of individual experience.

A *movement* is a commitment, on the part of one or more groups, to seek a certain social or political change. Such groups usually exist for the express purpose of pursuing this goal, although it may be loosely or ambiguously defined, especially if pursued simulta-neously by several competing groups, and may even be revised. A mature social or political movement consists of an inner core of leaders and members who identify with the organization, and an outer aggregation of sympathizers whose commitment is still qualified. A movement seeks to achieve its goals by mobilizing the support of a population and increasing the number of people who identify with it.

An *ideology* is the general understanding that is fundamental to the attitudes, actions, and responses of individuals within a particu-lar society or culture. All movements therefore have an underlying ideology, although this may be simply the dominant one in that culture, or a variant. Certain political or social movements are sup-ported by new or unique ideologies, that is, ones that differ sub-stantially or even radically from those generally operative; these are properly called ideological movements.

The independence movement in Quebec is an ideological movement in the sense that it is grounded in a distinct, if centuries-old ideology, that of survival, and premised on the new understanding that survival may require a substantial change in the present political structure.

Finally, since this book has been written chiefly for English-speaking readers, I have chosen to use the words *Separatism* and *Separatist* instead of the more accurate but unfamiliar and awkward-sounding terms *Independentism* and *Independentist*. To some ears, Separatism has distinctly destructive connotations, implying that there is an integral whole that is to be violated. It is impossible, they argue, to speak of separating something that is not whole; to use the term is to prejudice the discussion. This argument is well taken if the term *Separatism* is understood as deriving from the verb *to separate*. But it is also permissible, at least for American readers, to read it as a derivative of the adjective *separate*, as in separate cultures, and in this sense, it is possible to see in Separatism an affirmation of a fact that has existed for over 300 years. In any event, Separatism is aimed at discontinuing Quebec's present constitutional relationship with Canada, and the term is used here to denote both the general ideology of independence and the attitudes and behaviors that support it.

NOTES

1. The flag has been modified, but its design and colors remain basically the same. A mid–eighteenth–century banner had three gold fleurs-de-lys in each quadrant; one dating from the early twentieth century displays a fleur-de-lys pointing inward from each corner.

2. See, for example, Margaret Atwood, *Survival* (Toronto: House of Anansi Press, Ltd., 1972); John Sloan Dickey and Whitney H. Shepardson, *Canada and the American Presence: The United States Interest in an Independent Canada* (New York: New York University Press, 1975), especially chapters 1 and 5.

3. Mason Wade, *The French Canadians, 1760–1967*, Rev. ed. (Toronto: Macmillan of Canada, 1968), p. 1.

4. Ernest Schachtel, *Metamorphosis* (New York: Basic Books, 1959), p. 284.

5. Andrew M. Greeley, *Unsecular Man: The Persistence of Religion* (New York: Schocken Books, 1972).

6. Eric Hoffer, *The True Believer: Thoughts on the Nature of Mass Movements* (New York: Harper and Row, Perennial Library Edition, 1966), p. 25.

7. Harold D. Lasswell and Abraham Kaplan, *Power and Society* (New Haven, Conn.: Yale University Press, 1965).

8. Alfred de Grazia, *Politics for Better or Worse* (Glenview, Ill.: Scott, Foresman and Company, 1973), p. 49.

9. Lasswell and Kaplan, *Power and Society*, pp. 56–57.

2 • Collective Consciousness

Quebec's memory begins with the year 1534, when Jacques Cartier set out from the port of Saint-Malo in Brittany. The fishing grounds off the coast of Newfoundland and at the mouth of the Saint Lawrence were already favored by French fisherman; Cartier's mission was to establish a French claim to the North American continent. At Gaspé he erected a cross bearing the fleur-de-lys and the legend, *Vive le roi de France,* symbols that would recur frequently in Quebec's history. He returned to France with two Iroquois Indians and a report of vast resources in timber and wildlife and abundant fisheries, assets that would play an important role in the development of New France. The following year Cartier returned to explore the St. Lawrence, passed the winter near the present city of Quebec, and sailed for home in the spring. His quest had revealed neither precious minerals nor a passage to the Orient, and his discoveries were scarcely appreciated by François I, who was preoccupied with the political consolidation of France. In 1541 Cartier again sailed for the New World, this time as a principal in an ambitious effort to establish a permanent colony and base for further exploration. But the severity of the North American winter, difficulties with the Indians, and the failure to discover anything of material promise forced the abandonment of the settlement in 1543.[1]

As a result of a hostile environment and lack of interest from France, Quebec's first settlement did not survive. For the rest of the century France's presence in North America was limited to the fishing trade and to the fur trade which later developed. Not until 1608 was a permanent settlement established, after extensive exploration of the Saguenay and St. Lawrence rivers and the Atlantic coast, by Samuel de Champlain. This was Quebec; in 1611 another colony was founded at Montreal. Champlain was also responsible for bringing to New France the Recollect and Jesuit fathers, whose missionary and educational efforts became a continuing theme in the history of Quebec. Until Louis XIV took direct control, the Jesuits were the prime movers of the colony.[2]

By 1663, when Quebec was transferred to direct royal control, the mercantilist era was at its height. An absolute monarch, Louis XIV assumed control over all aspects of political, social, and economic policy. He was lured by Canada's vast wealth in fur, minerals, and fisheries; he was also interested in establishing on the North American continent a sizable French population that could sustain itself by means of an agricultural economy. The Company of New France had been, for the most part, unsuccessful in its efforts to develop a profitable fur trade or to increase the size of the settlement; Louis hoped to accomplish both. He saw in Quebec the opportunity to consolidate France's power in the New World. His minister, Colbert, saw colonization as an answer to the problem of burgeoning cities, unemployment and vagrancy. Into the vast expanse of lower Canada, therefore, he dispatched a few thousand men. Early marriages and large families were encouraged. The *filles du roi*—literally, daughters of the king, poor and orphaned girls of fourteen or fifteen who had been wards of the crown—were sent over as intended brides.[3] In 1675 the European population of Quebec numbered only 7,000. By 1760, when Quebec fell to the British, it had increased to approximately 70,000, due to a healthy birth rate and sporadic migration. More than 25,000 marriages and 138,000 births were recorded during this period. The frequency of intermarriage among the population of New France resulted in a correspondingly high degree of social cohesiveness along family lines and was an important integrating factor from the very beginning.[4]

In 1672 France again became involved in wars on the European continent. The promise of great riches had failed to materialize, while costs of administering the colony had risen steadily. Overpopulation, which a decade earlier had been resolved through colonization, was now a distinct asset to a king in need of large armies. Colbert now feared that France would be depopulated, and the policy of intensive colonization was discontinued.[5] Quebec's isolation from France had begun. The Church resumed its position as the single influential institution in the daily life of the colony. France's rule was still visible in the presence of the colonial governors, and of the military, who did not hesitate to enlist the young *habitant* in their wars with the British, but France's commitment to the colony had ceased. General Wolfe's victory in 1759 only made the situation permanent.

Even today, the Conquest is recalled as the critical event in Quebec's history. It is significant for two reasons. First, it is remembered as the event that sealed the fate of French Canada. It is because of the Conquest that Quebec is, constitutionally speaking, part of Canada today. Although the precise relationship has been altered several times, the Conquest marked its beginning. For this reason, many Quebecers have difficulty in accepting the Confederation established in 1867 as legitimate; it was based on conquest, they argue, and not on choice.[6] But the Conquest is also remembered as defeat and betrayal, the final step in the abandonment of New France by the mother country. In the winter of 1758–59, the governor of New France, the Marquis de Vaudreuil, vainly sent pleas for troops; he was ignored. As General Montcalm lay dying on September 13, 1759, he sent word to Vaudreuil to continue fighting, but instead, the Governor ordered a retreat. When the British offered them free passage back to France in British ships, the French soldiers were only too happy to go.[7] The Treaty of Paris, signed in 1763, offered repatriation to French civilians, but this time few took advantage of the opportunity. After several generations on North American soil, their commitment was to Quebec and to the ideology of national survival.

Quebec's uniqueness and cultural isolation on the North American continent are based not only on language and kinship but on the circumstances of settlement as well. As Kenneth D. McRae has pointed out, the English colonies were "offshoots of a society already divided within itself. French Canada was the closely controlled projection of a highly centralized regime." The tradition of dissent and protest played no role in the settlement of New France; indeed, after the arrival of the Jesuits, Protestants were barred from the colony.[8] Quebec's forefathers are remembered not as dissenters but as explorers, *coureurs de bois* (hunters and trappers), and *habitants* (settlers), whose survival could be equated with the increase of a glorious civilization.

The vast area claimed by France, the severity of Canadian winters, and the difficulties in communication combined to produce distinctive social patterns as early as the seventeenth century. Settlements, even in agricultural communities, followed a distinctively linear pattern, with houses close together, fronting on a river or road, and with properties running perpendicular to the river. This pattern, together with the community of interest resulting from a primitive agrarian economy, produced an extraordinary degree of solidarity within the community. It tended to render the *seigneurs,* or manor lords, obsolete and thereby to enhance the power of the Church at the expense of the state.[9]

The sociologist Marcel Rioux has commented, "Geography and history have combined to place Quebecers in an area completely dominated by two peoples of Anglo-Saxon descent: the Americans to the south, and the English Canadians to the west, to the east, and more or less everywhere in the territory of Quebec itself."[10] Yet the isolation of Quebec—and the historical integrity of her boundaries—has contributed significantly to her national and cultural survival. For nearly two centuries these boundaries assured a degree of cultural autonomy which Quebecers could take for granted. The ideology of survival and the issue of autonomy rarely came into conflict.

After the Conquest, Quebec's history bears the indelible imprint of Britain's efforts to incorporate two distinct cultures within a workable political system. In his 1965 manifesto, *Egalité ou Indépendance*, ("Equality or Independence"),[11] Daniel Johnson, premier of Quebec from 1966 to 1968, identifies five distinct constitutional experiences in the history of Quebec.

The first of these was the period immediately following the Conquest, when Quebec was ruled directly from Britain by royal proclamation and various ordinances. The king's representative, Governor James Murray, did not hesitate to praise the "uncommon generosity" of the conquerors in his dispatches to the British Colonial Office. Their gallantry, he said

> convinced these poor deluded people how grossly they had been imposed upon . . . the daily instances of lenity, the impartial justice which had been administered, so far beyond what they had formerly experienced, have so altered their opinion with regard to us . . . that, far from having the least design to emigrate into any other of the French colonies, their greatest dread is lest they should meet with the fate of the Acadians and be torn from their native country.[12]

Murray firmly believed that the defeat of the French had improved the lot of the people, but he was still apprehensive about the influence of the clergy, who, he felt, lacked sufficient respect for His Majesty. He was especially concerned about the Jesuits, whose "turbulent and intriguing genius," he feared, might "prompt them to play some trick," and he recommended their expulsion. Their estate, he argued, would provide the funds "to assist the people in rebuilding their Great Church [which] would much ingratiate their new Masters with them.[13]

Despite the efforts of Murray and his successor, Guy Carleton, to win the favor of the population, the government of a society essentially French in its traditions and culture by English laws proved unworkable. As early as 1768 Carleton informed the colonial office that the government of *Canadiens* (French Canadians) by unfamiliar, unpublished laws was "contrary to their temperament, to the location of the colony and to the interests of Great Britain." Accordingly, the Quebec Act of 1774 reestablished French laws and freedom of worship.

But this experiment proved as unsatisfactory as the first. The English minority chafed at being governed by French law. It was apparent even then, Johnson comments, "that there were two cultural communities in Canada, two nations as yet embryonic but already so different that it was neither just nor efficient to govern them the same way."[14] A third attempt was therefore launched.

The Constitutional Act of 1791 divided the country into two colonies, Upper Canada, whose borders corresponded roughly with those of present-day Ontario, and Lower Canada, formerly New France. The act also instituted representative government in each colony, raising for the first time the question of an official language in Quebec's legislature. The principle of two nations, which was to reappear in the British North America Act of 1867, dates from this period. Johnson notes that in 1791 the population of Upper Canada numbered only about 10,000. "The division, therefore was not based on numbers, but on principle."[15]

This constitutional experiment lasted fifty years. It corresponded with the end of the *ancien régime* and the severing of cultural ties with France, and a corresponding growth in the influence of the Church. Rioux comments: "Two concepts of France develop; the good France, pre-1789, and the bad, post-revolutionary France. After the Conquest, Quebec is organized as a traditional society, a folk society, but it still retains some ties with the great tradition of France. Her overall culture, then, is based on oral tradition, but some connections are maintained with the rest of the Western world, thanks primarily to the clergy."[16] The period was a definitive one in the development of Quebec's national consciousness. Attitudes formed during this time about the English-speaking population, and the reliability and legitimacy of their institutions, can be recognized as a continuing theme in Quebec nationalism. Because there was no indigenous upper class, the French Canadians lacked investment capital and soon fell under the economic domination of the English.[17] The result was a "division along these lines into "haves' and 'have nots,' which lasted for nearly a century," and conflict between mercantilism and traditionalism.[18] Parliamentary government only served to reinforce negative attitudes toward the English. Despite an almost universal suffrage, the governmental system was dominated by an appointive hierarchy, which resulted in inadequate representation for French Canadians within their own territory. The magistracy and the civil service were also dominated by the English-speaking minority. This experience was seen as proof that English institutions were unreliable and not to be trusted. The paradoxical coincidence of a territorial division of powers on an ethnic basis, with the political and economic domination of one group over the other, may be seen as the root of Quebec's alienation from the Canadian system.

Separatism may first be observed in the 1830s, when adverse economic conditions led to open conflict between the legislature and the governor. Unrest had been mounting since 1832, when the newly organized British-American Land Company began buying up existing farmland for British immigrants. The failure to open up the crown lands, where the *habitant* might have been able to continue farming, and the resulting shortage of arable land, caused an intense speculation that resulted in severe economic dislocations. By 1837, according to Fernand Ouellet, "misery and discontent reign everywhere. The slight hopes entertained for the coming harvest are deceived; the situation grows worse instead of better. Moreover, the crisis of 1837 does not concern agriculture only; it is general"[19] In the National Assembly, Louis-Joseph Papineau, leader of the Parti Patriote, blamed the English Canadian hierarchy and renewed his demand for constitutional revision. In London, the Colonial Office agreed to minor reforms but rejected Papineau's call for an elected upper house. In addition, it refused to dissolve the British American Land Company, and it revoked the legislature's power to grant or withhold revenues from the governor. The resistance of the Patriotes was, in the beginning, nonviolent. In April a boycott of imported, and therefore dutiable, goods was organized. "The sources of revenue must be dried up," read an editorial in *La Minerve*. "The vaults will empty; the thieves will find nothing more there. Then England will listen to reason." But the economic action soon became political. During the spring and summer, as the crisis continued, public meetings were organized. Skirmishes with the British inevitably followed, and by November the rebellion was in full swing. On December 14, the revolt's bloodiest clash occurred at Saint-Eustache, and a number of the Patriote leaders were taken into custody. On the following day, the neighboring village of Saint-Benoit was pillaged and destroyed by the British, despite its surrender upon the arrival of the troops.[20] This was the last episode of the revolt. Yet, despite its comparatively short duration, the Rebellion of 1837 and its political aftermath may be seen as a watershed in Quebec's history. In 1841, Parliament, acting upon Lord Durham's recommendation that Lower Canada be assimilated both politically and culturally into the English-speaking population, reunited the two colonies. This fourth constitutional experiment lasted only until 1867, but it ushered in a period that was to last until the late 1950s. Rioux observes,

> After 1840 the picture changes completely. Even the most committed French Canadians are filled with despair. Their task is no longer to lead their people to independence, but to struggle against assimilation and anglicization. . . . With the support of Durham, the clergy becomes the chief spokesman of the Quebec people; it will define an ideology of preservation rather than an ideology of independence.[21]

Ultimately, the revolt of the Patriotes, the Durham report, and the Act of Union had the effect of forcing Quebec back on her own resources and institutions. The ideology of survival resulted in the cultural hegemony of the Church and a conservative nationalism that stressed the virtues of tradition over the present needs, and the traditional values of deference to authority, thrift, humility, and even sacrifice. After 1841, those political, economic, and cultural needs which had momentarily found expression in a separatist movement were held in abeyance for well over a century.

The fifth constitutional act, the British North America Act of 1867, failed to change this process. On an institutional level, the principle of two nations was reestablished. Its net effect, however, was to preserve the substructure that existed at the time of Confederation. Mason Wade notes that "the question of survival for the French Canadians was brought more to the fore by Confederation than at any time since the Conquest." For the first time they were substantially outnumbered by the English-speaking population, and "the defensiveness aroused by this fact was enough to breed a strong spirit of reaction."[22] The most significant provisions of the BNA Act, for this analysis, were section 133, which guaranteed the use of either French or English in the Parliament at Ottawa and in the Quebec legislature, and in the federal and Quebec courts, and section 93, which gave the provinces exclusive control over education, and guaranteed the continuance of denominational schools. Together, these two sections reinforced the inherent "separateness" of French Canadian culture.[23]

With Confederation, Quebec became one of four provinces. Although the new union offered important constitutional guarantees, such as a legislature of its own and fixed representation in federal institutions, the two nations principle was placed in jeopardy from the very beginning. No issue provoked more heated argument than that of English-Canadian domination of the new federal system. The problem reached a crisis level in 1885, with the execution of Louis Riel.

Riel, a Métis, had led a rebellion in the newly established province of Manitoba against the extension of Eastern, Anglo-Canadian domination into the Western territories. The Métis, or half-blooded Indians, were also descendants of French- or English-speaking settlers, but by the mid-nineteenth century they had developed an identity of their own and had begun to consider themselves a new nation. Their social and political institutions reflected both the traditions of their Indian and immigrant forebears and the exigencies of life at the frontier. Land divisions there followed the riverstrip pattern popular in early Quebec; this became a particularly heated issue when the federal government decided to survey the same lands according to the square-section system. As a result, property titles were thrown into disarray.[24] This was but one of the many disputes that led to increasing unrest among the Métis and culminated in the North-West Rebellion of 1885.

Riel was obviously emotionally unstable. His speech was often incoherent. A religious fanatic, he believed himself a prophet; at times he called himself Elijah or David. Nevertheless, he possessed a charismatic, if somewhat rabid appeal, capable of arousing his Métis compatriots and terrifying the officials in Ottawa. In March 1885, he established a provincial government of the Métis, with himself as president, called for a "war of extermination," and began a series of raids against his "enemies." Riel's insurrection lasted just over two months, and he was hanged in Regina, Saskatchewan, in November 1885. But by then his name had become a rallying cry for French Canadians. Within days of his execution there were mass demonstrations in Quebec; the largest one, held in Montreal on November 22, attracted a crowd of 40,000 people. Three platforms were set up, and from them Quebec's leaders, Liberals and Conservatives alike, condemned the central government. Honoré

Mercier, the leader of the moderate Liberals, spoke movingly of "Riel, our brother . . . victim of fanaticism and treason." His death was "a blow to the heart of our race, but above all [to] the cause of justice and humanity, which represented in all languages and sanctified by all religious beliefs, begged mercy for the prisoner of Regina, our poor brother of the North-West." Mercier then called for the formation of a new political party, capable of uniting all French Canadians in their outrage against the government.[25] Although he never succeeded in his plan to organize such a party on the federal level, his Parti National swept into power in Quebec eleven months later.

Riel's name is still preserved in song and in legend. His death was understood—and is still remembered—as the supreme example of the fate of French Canadians in a federal system dominated by the English. He was tried by an English judge, before a jury of six Englishmen. But his death also symbolized the exclusion from Canada's future—by violence, if necessary—of all that did not conform with Anglo-Saxon standards. After this it became clear that the French presence in North America would be confined to Quebec, and in the next fifty years the language rights of French Canadians outside Quebec were progressively limited.

In 1935 Canon Groulx, in his study of French education in Canada, summarized the history of French Canadian education rights outside Quebec from 1860 to 1930.

1864—*Nova Scotia:* French-speaking Catholic Acadians are forbidden to have French schools.

1871—*New Brunswick:* Catholic schools are closed and the teaching of French (and in French) is forbidden in the public schools.

1877—*Prince Edward Island:* Catholic and French schools become outlawed.

1890—*Manitoba:* Separate (Catholic) schools are outlawed and the teaching of French (and in French) is forbidden at the secondary level.

1892—*Northwest Territories (including what is now Alberta and Saskatchewan):* Teaching in French is outlawed in public schools and Catholic Schools are prohibited.

1905—*Alberta and Saskatchewan:* The regulations of 1892 (Northwest Territories) are confirmed.

1912—*Keewatin:* Denominational (Catholic) schools are suppressed and the teaching of French is forbidden.

1915—*Ontario:* By regulation (regulation No. 17), French is outlawed in Ontario schools.

1916—*Manitoba:* The teaching of French is forbidden at all levels.

1930—*Sasketchewan:* The teaching of French is prohibited even outside school hours.[26]

Although article 133 of the British North America Act permitted the use of the Franch language by any person, the federal government was, for all intents and purposes, unilingual until the late 1960s, when the Liberal party, under Pierre Trudeau, instituted a policy of bilingualism.

A further change in Quebec's formal relations with the British Empire occurred in 1931, with the Statute of Westminster, which effectively ended Parliament's power to make laws concerning Canada. The event was hailed by many French Canadians as the achievement of independence from Britain after nearly two centuries of domination. In effect, it was to focus the issue of French Canadian nationalism on Dominion-provincial relations. It paved the way for the issue of constitutional revision that arose in the 1950s and for the consideration of more radical solutions in Quebec.

Traditional nationalism was as much a power structure as an identity. Though its legacy—the preservation of a national consciousness—was to reappear in Separatism, its appeal was to an entrenched and shrinking power structure. With the end of World War II and the return to power of the conservative Union Nationale party in Quebec, the old nationalism came face to face with an emerging "Canadian" consciousness. Fifteen years were to pass, and a new generation would emerge, before a new ideology would issue from this conflict.

Change was not broadly seen or felt, in the period before 1960, but new power bases were developing. Industrialization, full employment, and foreign investment irrevocably changed the social structure of Quebec. The traditional family and parochial orientations began to dissolve, and many French Canadians realized for the first time that their cultural isolation put them at an economic disadvantage. Provincial autonomy in the fields of education and culture had for years meant that the individual did not have to face problems of cultural conflict. Industrialization also increased the significance of certain segments of society—chiefly labor, the universities, and the intellectuals—and foretold the decline of the traditional sources of influence—the Church, the professional and managerial class, and above all the Union Nationale and its conservative ideological stand, and prepared the way for the Quiet Revolution and its turbulent aftermath.[27]

The changing expectations of the working class were accompanied by a basic change in the orientation of the Church, which was beginning to abandon its traditional role as custodian of an ancient faith for issues of social justice. The Asbestos Strike of 1949 was settled chiefly through the efforts of the Archbishop of Quebec, who in a pastoral letter the following year set down principles for both labor and industry and indicated the Church's intention to concentrate on social issues. The increased support of the Church coincided with a growing rift between labor and the Union Nationale, whose interest in attracting foreign investment depended on the availability of cheap labor. In 1956 the Catholic syndicates of Quebec joined the new Canadian Labor Congress, and in the Murdochville strike of 1957 they demanded labor conditions equal to those prevailing in the rest of Canada.[28] These developments were indicative of a new and widespread attitude that Quebec could "catch up" politically, economically, and socially with the other provinces.

New intellectual currents can also be traced to the period of the 1950s, although their impact was not felt until after 1960. The liberal review, *Cité Libre*, founded by Trudeau, first appeared in 1950. A Faculty of Social Sciences was founded at Laval University, and throughout Quebec educational opportunities were beginning to expand. The traditional attitudes about ethnic discrimination and economic exploitation by the English faltered, and for the first time many French Canadians saw themselves as partners in Confederation.[29] These new expectations were reinforced by the return to power in France of General de Gaulle and the rapproachement with the Fifth Republic and by the recognition of independence (with its implications of political viability) for former French-speaking colonies. These two international developments supported a feeling of pride in the "French" heritage and a sense of cultural equality.

A final development was the elevation of the Papacy of Cardinal Roncalli, who became John XXIII. More than any other factor, Vatican II speeded the trend toward secularization and helped to put an end to the traditional authority of the Church. The faltering of the traditional authority structure in Quebec society created a need for a new institution capable of articulating and directing the wants of French Canadians. This vacuum would ultimately be filled by the independence movement.

The Quiet Revolution is the name commonly given to the period between 1960 and 1966. It begins with the defeat of the Union

Nationale in 1960 and ends with the defeat of Quebec's Liberal party. It was characterized by political and administrative reforms and above all by the spread of new attitudes:

> 1960 marks the beginning of Quebecers' reconciliation with themselves. For a century they had striven to preserve their heritage; more recently, they had tried to catch up with the other North Americans; now they asked themselves if they did not have some original contribution to make to the world of human societies.[30]

The Quiet Revolution profoundly changed the perception of national survival. For the first time in history, survival could be seen as innovation. This new attitude challenged the traditional, more passive view of survival that was based upon the affirmation of the group's values and social and cultural characteristics. Garigue ascribes this change to the rising consciousness of the group and the growing awareness of the needs that confronted it. Survival, in the form of "dynamic adaptation," creates change through "the desire to introduce within the group those elements necessary to assure survival."[31] The notion of autonomy underwent a corresponding change, from emphasis on cultural preservation to more aggressive demands for power. These changed perceptions would alter the course of Quebec's history. In the early 1960s they produced new enthusiasm and optimism concerning Quebec's partnership with English-speaking Canada. Such was the Quiet Revolution. When its promise failed to materialize, the search for an alternative solution began.

The period that began with the Quiet Revolution witnessed the breaking of the "monolithic conservative ideology of the French Canadian elites, which [was] strongly rooted in religious and educational institutions and closely tied with their constant preoccupation with nationalist concerns."[32] By the early 1960s there was little to inhibit the development of a new leadership that would unite the left. The failure of the Union Nationale leadership had coincided with the ascendancy of certain segments of society whose collective goals were best expressed by the Liberal party. There were thus three ideologies competing in the early 1960s: the new Liberal ideology, the old Conservatism, and Separatism, which first appeared as a social movement in 1957, with the founding of the Alliance Laurentienne. The politics of the late 1960s were increasingly shaped by the conflict among these groups over the issues of autonomy and progress.

Separatism in recent years has not been without occasional violence. In the period after 1961, when Frantz Fanon's *Les Damnés de la terre (The Wretched of the Earth)*[33] was published in French, various groups began considering Quebec's position as a victim of colonialism and economic exploitation by both Canada and the United States. This type of Separatism is internationalist rather than nationalist; it is movingly described by Pierre Vallières in *White Niggers of America: The Precocious Autobiography of a Quebec Terrorist.*[34] For Vallières, the history of Quebec is a nightmare best remembered only so that it is not repeated. Rather than using this past to validate their culture, the people of Quebec should use its lessons toward structuring an independent and socialist future. These groups differed in their degree of militancy, but they all agreed on the need for liberation. The Armée de la Libération du Québec (ALQ) was an organization that made threats and carried out bombing attacks; the Front de Libération du Québec (FLQ) was better known, especially after 1970, when the kidnapping and murder of Pierre Laporte made it the focus of worldwide attention.

The October Crisis and the invocation of the War Measures Act had the effect of forcing underground the more radical Separatist groups, and increasing the visibility of the Parti Québécois, whose leaders urged the government of Quebec to negotiate. The murder of Laporte appalled and repelled most Quebecers. At the same time, the severity of Ottawa's reaction and the failure of the Liberals to mitigate Ottawa's position in the developing crisis alienated many of them. The crisis increased their distrust of Canada's peremptory attitudes toward the internal affairs of Quebec, and for those who still had hoped for a political solution, it enhanced the appeal of the Parti Québécois.[35]

Economic factors have also played a significant role in the development of Separatism in Quebec. Historically there have been two parallel economic systems in Quebec. In 1973, a provincial commission on the status of the French language in Quebec documented an extreme stratification along linguistic lines. This in turn promoted the exclusive utilization of one language or the other in certain sectors of the economy, to the extent that there were two essentially complete and exclusive networks of communication. Public administration, social services, and small business were dominated by *francophones*, or persons whose maternal language is French, while the large corporations, public utilities, and finance were dominated by the *anglophones*.[36]

One widely respected scholar, an economist who asked that he not be identified, sees Separatism as a direct result of the economic dominance of English-speaking over French-speaking Canadians. The issue of national and cultural survival is, in this view, a "phantom" created by the Quebec bourgeoisie. In struggling to maintain its position, this class, composed chiefly of merchants, professionals, politicians, and clergy, established itself as the protector of the masses, thus gaining a powerful ally with which to threaten English Canadians.

The resurgence of Separatism can be traced to the expansion of the bourgeoisie in the period after 1960. As a result of economic prosperity and increased educational opportunities, a much larger segment of the population, chiefly under thirty-five years of age, is seeking to divide the portion of the gross national product that the English Canadians are willing to concede. The failure of the economy to expand rapidly enough to meet the aspirations of this class has created, in this view, a wave of dissatisfaction and alienation which has forced them to seek alternative political and economic solutions. While the mobility of this class makes it easy for them to espouse Separatism, the same is not true for the mass of the population. Those lacking skills or a knowledge of English have no access to job markets elsewhere in North America. Unlike the bourgeoisie, they would have no effective alternatives should Separatism prove economically nonviable. For this reason, the Parti Québécois launched a broad campaign to convince the working class of the economic advantages of independence. A minimum wage and the equalization of income were two widely publicized features of the 1973 and 1976 campaigns. The success of Separatism may well depend on the ability of the educated classes to the workers the proposition that independence is economically necessary.

Separatism, in the contemporary political context of Quebec, is thus a constellation of attitudes with one unifying theme, independence, and one significant organ, the Parti Québécois. Those who espouse Separatism may be classified into two broad categories: those who vote for the PQ and those who are members. The degree and nature of independence sought ranges from "total" independence, meaning a severing of all political and economic ties with Canada and the United States, to "special status," or "sovereignty-association." Most Separatists do not seem to care that their position differs from that currently taken by the Party Québécois; their main concern is in gaining the power to make a collective decision on their own future. Most essentially, Separatists are concerned with survival, not only as a nation, but as a culture with a specific value system which itself is the product of their national experience. Separatism sustains itself in Quebec because it addresses itself not only to the issue of survival, but to a range of current needs as well. The success of Separatism as an ideological movement, then, is based not only on its intellectual appeal, but on a culturally specific value system.

NOTES

1. Mason Wade, *The French Canadians 1760–1967* (Toronto: Macmillan of Canada, 1968), 1:1–9.

2. Ibid., pp. 10–15.

3. Kenneth D. McRae, "The Structure of Canadian History," in Louis Hartz, *The Founding of New Societies* (New York: Harcourt Brace and World, 1964), pp. 220–21; Wade, pp. 16–18.

4. Philippe Garigue, *La Vie familiale des Canadiens français* (Montreal: Les Presses de l'Université de Montreal, 1970), p. 15.

5. Wade, *French Canadians*, p. 20.

6. For a discussion of the issue of legitimacy and the relations between the two cultures, see Gerard F. Rutan, "Two Views of the Concept of Sovereignty: Canadian and Canadien," *Western Political Quarterly* 24 (1971): 456–66.

7. Stephen Usherwood, "Conquered Canada: General James Murray's Impressions, 1762," *History Today* 29 (1979): 350.

9. Marcel Rioux, *Quebec in Question*, trans. by James Boake (Toronto: James Lewis and Samuel, 1971), pp. 14–16.

10. Ibid., p. 5.

11. Daniel Johnson, *Egalité ou indépendance* Montreal: Editions de l'Homme, 1966.

12. Governor Murray to Lord Egremont, June 1762, as quoted in Usherwood, p. 352.

13. Ibid., p. 355.

14. Johnson, *Egalité ou indépendance*, p. 27.

15. Ibid., p. 2.

16. Rioux, *Quebec in Question*, p. 36.

17. Ibid., pp. 39–40; Wade, *French Canadians*, p. 23.

18. Wade, *French Canadians*, p. 24.

19. Fernand Ouellet, *Histoire économique et sociale du Québec* (Montreal: Fides, 1966), pp. 421–22, as quoted in Rioux, p. 51.

20. Wade, *French Canadians*, pp. 178–79.

21. Rioux, *Quebec in Question*, p. 65.

22. Wade, *French Canadians*, p. 331.

23. This is the opinion of the *Report of the Commission on the Position of the French Language and on Language Rights in Quebec* (Gendron Report), Book 2, Language Rights (Montreal: L'Editeur officiel du Québec 1972).

24. Wade, *French Canadians*, p. 394.

25. R. Rumilly, *Histoire de la Province de Québec*, 5: 121, as quoted in Wade, p. 417.

26. *L'Enseignement Français au Canada* (Montreal: Granger Frères, 1935), as quoted in Bernard, p. 27.

27. Wade, *French Canadians*, p. 1107.

28. Ibid., pp. 1108–10.

29. Ibid., pp. 1111–16.

30. Rioux, *Quebec in Question*, p. 76.

31. Garigue, *La Vie famiale*, pp. 30–32.

32. Maurice Pinard, *The Rise of a Third Party* (Englewood Cliffs, N.J.: Prentice-Hall, 1971), p. 99.

33. Frantz Fanon, *Les Damnés de la terre* Paris: Maspéro, 1961.

34. Pierre Vallières, *White Niggers of America: The Precocious Autobiography of a Quebec Terrorist* (New York: Monthly Review, 1972).

35. The view that Trudeau acted too hastily was widely expressed by both Separatists and Federalists in private conversations. See also Gérard Pelletier, *The October Crisis* (Toronto: McClelland and Stewart, 1971), and John T. Saywell *Quebec 70: A Documentary History* (Toronto: University of Toronto Press, 1971).

36. Gendron Report, 2: 125–26.

3 • The Politics of Survival

When the Parti Québécois gained power in 1976, it was the fourth time a new nationalist party had won a majority of seats in Quebec's National Assembly.[1] All three of the PQ's predecessors had attempted to free Quebec from the domination of Canada's English-speaking majority; all three had ultimately failed in their attempts to change Quebec's constitutional and political status. But there were two important differences between the 1976 election and the previous ones: The Parti Québécois rejected violence and it clearly advocated independence as essential to national survival. The Parti Patriote had resorted to armed provocation in an effort to achieve its objectives; violent repression followed, and the party disbanded and disappeared for good. Papineau's experience was remembered as a lesson in survival: play along and things may be tolerable; try to change matters and you'll be defeated; try to leave and you're done for. This attitude prevailed for well over a century. It was supported by Quebec's traditional elite and by the Anglo-Canadians as well, and by the experience of the Parti National and the Union Nationale. Until the advent of the Parti Québécois, no major political party dared call for independence.

In January 1887 the Parti National, led by Honoré Mercier, took office. Mercier's party had been formed in the moment of defensiveness and reaction that followed Riel's execution in November 1885. Its electoral victory was understood in Quebec as a response to the progressive undermining of French language and education rights in the other provinces. But elsewhere it was regarded quite differently. Mercier's party had as its hero a man who was at best a madman and at worst a traitor; to the Anglo-Canadians it represented a return to the lawlessness of 1837. The *Toronto Mail* warned that French Canadians were "now seeking to compel us to recognise their right to suspend the operation of the law when a representative of their race is in the toils," and it darkly suggested that it might become necessary to dissolve the confederation and reconquer Quebec.[2]

Mercier had hoped to found a French Canadian party at the national level; he also had plans for revising the British North America Act to improve the constitutional and economic status of French Canadians and of Quebec. But once in power, he found his own electorate unwilling to support him in a firm stand against Ottawa, and he had to curtail sharply his requests for provincial autonomy. The Conservative government in Ottawa rejected even these pleas. Mercier's politics had provoked a backlash aimed at discrediting both the leaders and the program of the Parti National, and in the end this policy was successful. The party was defeated after five years in office, and disappeared with Mercier's death two years later.[3]

While his government was in power, Mercier did not advocate separation. The Parti National had been formed to advance the rights of French Canadians within the Confederation, and although a small number of party activists had favored secession at the very beginning, there was little support for their position. To call openly for independence would have been to risk political suicide. But by 1893, Mercier no longer had anything to lose. In an address to 6,000 people in Montreal, he let out his true feelings:

> In undertaking this considerable task which I have imposed upon myself, I wished to show you what our country could be, this Canada, dear to all our hearts. I have done all that I could to open up new horizons for you, and by making you see them, pushed you towards the realization of our natural destinies. You have colonial dependence, I offer you independence; you have shame and misery, I offer you fortune and prosperity; you are only a colony ignored by the entire world, I offer you the opportunity of becoming a great people, recognized and respected among nations.
>
> Men, women and children, it is for you to choose; you can remain slaves under colonial status, or become independent and free, among other peoples who invite you to the banquet of nations.[4]

But for all his effusive nationalism, Mercier failed to rally Quebecers to the cause of independence. They had seen his earlier, moderate policies defeated by the federal government, and the lesson of Papineau told them that accommodation was the only realistic means of dealing with Ottawa. By this time, Quebec had found a new leader in Wilfred Laurier, whose appeal to Canadian unity would carry him to victory in the Canadian elections of 1896.

In 1936 the people of Quebec again elected a nationalist government. The Union Nationale, under the leadership of Maurice Duplessis, came to power fifty years after its predecessor, the Parti National, and it remained in power for all but five of the next twenty-four years. It represented the merger of the provincial Conservative party and a group that had broken with the provincial Liberals. Like its predecessor, the Union Nationale was formed during a period of strife, but this time the crisis was chiefly an economic one. The party appealed to the working class, which had been hard-hit by the Depression, not because of its ideological position, but because it offered them a means of voicing their dissatisfaction with the reigning Liberal party and held out the hope of relieving their economic misery. In his efforts to forge a working-class majority, Duplessis avoided taking extreme positions. His nationalism was one of quiet conservatism characterized by an idealization of Quebec's traditional society.[5] According to Rioux's account, Duplessis "put into practice the conservative doctrines which had existed in Quebec for many years. Totally pragmatic, suspicious of intellectuals and ideologists, Duplessis espoused the most conservative of politics in the name of Quebec autonomy and peasant good sense."[6]

Duplessis's reforms were, for the most part, nonexistent. The modest promises of his 1936 campaign remained, by his choice, unfulfilled. He did officially adopt the *fleurdelisé*, the flag Quebecers recognize today, and he somewhat hesitantly established a provincial income tax, but he failed to take a strong position on social issues, or to expand the role of government, and he made no effort to improve Quebec's constitutional status. Those who could not reconcile his conservative nationalism with the idea of autonomy left the party in 1938; some of them even called for independence. But this type of nationalism proved no match for Duplessis's variety, and, like their predecessors, they attracted little support and their party, the Action Liberale Nationale, soon disappeared.[7]

Not until the 1960s did large numbers of Quebecers seriously reconsider the idea of independence. It is significant that the independence movement, when it finally did emerge, was not a political but an educational one. By calling Quebecers not to political action but to a rational, intellectual consideration of their situation, it directed its primary appeal to their intellectual needs. By eschewing, for the time being, political action, it opened up the possibility of exploring freely present needs and available options without immediate commitment.

The first important organization produced by this movement was the Alliance Laurentienne, founded in January 1957. At its height it numbered no more than 4,000 members. It attempted to raise interest in the independence issue through the publication of a review, *Laurentie,* and a number of books on independence. The Alliance Laurentienne approached the issue of national sovereignty in much the same way as René Lévesque would a decade later. Independence was presented not as an end in itself but as the only viable means for ensuring that those elements most intrinsic to Quebec's identity and sense of worth, chiefly language, religion, and tradition, would be preserved. Its membership consisted chiefly of students, militant Catholic nationalists, some professionals, and right-wing intellectuals; it was too narrowly conservative to attract a broad following.[8] It failed to address current problems in terms relevant to the average Quebecer and was unable to evoke a response sufficient to keep it growing.

In 1960 about thirty members of the Alliance Laurentienne, dissatisfied with the extreme right-wing ideas of its leadership, withdrew and formed a new organization, the Rassemblement pour l'Indépendance Nationale. This new organization, known popularly as the RIN, was to become the major organ of the independence movement in the period preceding the emergence of the Parti Québécois. Together with the Ralliement National (RN), a more conservative group formed in 1966, it would make the issue of independence a matter of serious concern for all Quebecers.

The RIN was, in the beginning, loosely structured. In keeping with its name, *rassemblement,* or assembly, it accommodated a wide range of political orientations. In its early years it served admirably as a forum for the discussion of topics and issues relating to independence. Its members were, according to its first president, André d'Allemagne, "entirely free to express and assert as individuals their ideas and convictions about questions dealing with internal politics, religion, economic theories and social doctrines." Once again, most of the group were young; a comparatively high proportion were students, and the membership included also intellectuals, writers, artists, actors, and civil servants. But unlike the Alliance Laurentienne, the RIN in its earliest years welcomed all comers.[9] In 1961 Montreal's two principal newspapers published the results of surveys in the independence issue. On March 18, *La Presse* reported that 45 percent "favored separatism," and on June 10 *Le Devoir* reported 75.2 percent of the population in sympathy with the movement. In September, Marcel Chaput published his best-selling *Why I Am a Separatist,*[10] and two months later his suspension (from his position as a chemist) by the National Defense Research Board became a cause célèbre. These events were followed by a dramatic increase in membership.

After 1962, however, the RIN began to change. A provincial election, called unexpectedly that year, presented it with an opportunity to test its appeal via the polls. The need to adopt a political program thus brought to an abrupt end the period of easy ambiguity with which it had begun. In its first political program, the RIN proclaimed itself "French, free, democratic and humanist." It emphasized the need to strengthen French culture, a position usually associated with conservative political movements. Yet at the same time the RIN took a position which identified it as secular in the extreme: it ended compulsory religious instruction in the public schools. The program was brief, but radical for its day, and it marked the RIN as an "organization of the left."[11]

During the following year, structural changes within the RIN ensured that this commitment would be maintained. The old assembly format, which had encouraged participation from people representing a broad spectrum of political beliefs, was abandoned in favor of a representative system. An executive committee was introduced. The overall result of these changes was that for the first time the party's leaders could count on the support they needed to shape the policy of the organization.

Several other pro-independence organizations, including the violent FLQ, made their appearance during the 1960s. The changes in the RIN led to the departure of nearly a third of its members in 1963. More of the conservatives left the following year to form the Regroupement National, which described itself as a political party committed to independence by democratic and peaceful means. In 1966 the Regroupement merged with another group, the Ralliement Créditiste, to form the Ralliement National. By 1966 there existed two well-developed pro-independence political parties, one to the left and one to the right. The RIN called for the separation of Quebec from Canada; the RN, preferring to frame its appeal in less drastic-sounding terms, advocated "associate states." These two alternatives have persisted despite the later integration of these groups within the Parti Québécois. Despite their differences, these two parties together constituted a force which, if still too small to anticipate a serious role within the Quebec legislature, was nonetheless capable of determining the results of the election. Together they won nine percent of the vote in the 1966 provincial election, drawing most of their support from new voters or from the Liberal party. The Union Nationale, by a narrow margin of seats, was once again in power.[12]

During this period, 1966–1970, two events occurred which led to the founding, in October 1968, of the Parti Québécois, and ultimately to its electoral victory in November 1976. The first was Charles de Gaulle's dramatic *"Vive le Québec libre,"* uttered in July 1967, and his subsequent endorsement of the independence movement. Support doubled; in addition, many who had secretly favored it now let their feelings be known. Perhaps the most dramatic revelation occurred on the floor of the National Assembly when François Aquin, a Liberal, fervently confessed, "After having known the occupation of the conqueror, the tutelage of the foreigners and betrayal from within, the people of Quebec now consider the state of Quebec to be the only tool for its progress."[13] The second event occurred at the annual convention of Quebec's Liberal party on September 18, 1967: René Lévesque, a former television commentator, a member of the Assembly since 1960, and one of the most respected personalities within the party, introduced a resolution calling for an independent Quebec in an economic association with Canada. When the party rejected it, Lévesque and several other influential Liberals left, although they continued to represent their constituencies as independents. In the following weeks Lévesque was courted by both the RIN and the RN. He tried to negotiate a union of his own group with the RIN, but he could not get them to accept his proposals for economic cooperation with Canada and the protection of English-language rights.[14]

From the very start Lévesque appears to have been seriously concerned with assuring the credibility of his organization. The experiences of Papineau, Mercier, and even Duplessis had proven how vulnerable to depreciation by a hostile federal government a nationalist party could be. Having explicitly called for independence—albeit with close economic ties to Canada—he could well contemplate the risks he faced in addressing his proposals to the people of Quebec. Like his predecessors, he was a man of considerable political stature. He had embarked on a career in politics after a successful one in the media; he had served in three cabinet-level positions. His espousal of the independence movement had added significantly to its appeal. Yet the potential for antagonism and quarreling among three pro-independence parties was capable of dividing and discrediting the movement without any help from Ottawa. Lévesque faced a serious dilemma: how to assume leadership of the existing independence movement, thus giving it added respectability, while avoiding the interparty combat which would undoubtedly weaken and discredit it.

His strategy was to form a transitional organization, the Mouvement Souveraineté Association, or Sovereignty-Association Movement, which became known as the MSA. This would serve as an umbrella for the existing groups; a political party would be organized later. At the MSA's founding congress in November 1967, Lévesque voiced his plea for the union of all pro-independence forces, especially the RIN and the RN, within the MSA. He also took a position that permanently set the movement on a moderate course in calling for a trade and monetary union with Canada.

Lévesque spent the next months touring Quebec and explaining his position. In January 1968 his book, *Option Québec (An Option for Quebec)*[15] was published. Lévesque took as a starting point not only the ideology but the reality of survival, and argued that the resulting constitutional crisis could be solved only through increased acceptance of responsibilities on the part of Quebec. The rewards for continuing the "fantastic adventure" begun nearly three centuries before were great: most important, in Lévesque's view, was the sense of well-being and even joy in being Quebecers. The penalties for abandoning it would be severe: "To be unable to live as ourselves, as we should live, in our own language and according to our own ways, would be like living without an arm or a leg—or perhaps a heart."[16]

To continue the adventure would require self-respect. Belief in the value of "belonging" was primary; faith in the "capacity to do the job ourselves" and "accept our responsibilities" were also essential. The conscious acceptance of Quebec's history and values, and the intellectual satisfaction of finding a solution for the future were further rewards outlined by Lévesque. And, although his proposals called for drastic political and economic changes, the object of affection remained constant and reassuring—Quebec. Quite apart from the solution itself, then, Lévesque's option presented a compelling appeal in terms of the traditional values in Quebec society. It reconciled the ideology of survival by joining it with a call for political sovereignty and economic self-sufficiency.

Lévesque's proposals are significant mainly because of their role in launching the Parti Québécois. They begin with the affirmation of the two-nations, or "two-majorities" theory, and the rejection of federalism as unworkable where one nation is substantially outnumbered, in terms of both population and territorial division of

power. The viability of Quebec requires certain constitutional safe-
guards that will ensure its ability to function. Lévesque refers to
this as "the power for unfettered action" in the fields of citizenship,
immigration, employment, mass culture, international relations,
social security and welfare, employment, language, education and
cultural affairs. In sum, Quebec must get for itself "the complete
mastery of every last area of basic collective decision-making. . . .
This means that Quebec must become sovereign as soon as possible."[17] The result would be a new Canadian union, which would
be mutually beneficial. English Canada would be released from the
centrifugal forces and constitutional dilemmas imposed by the present bi-national structure, and Quebec would achieve the "full
political liberty" which is its due."[18] Lévesque believes that Quebec
is more than self-sufficient economically, and that the present federal revenue arrangements are unduly costly for the province. A
monetary union and common-market system would be far more
beneficial to Quebec than the centralized economy desired by Ottawa.[19]

In emphasizing Quebec's need for economic self-sufficiency,
Lévesque continued the tradition of economic nationalism formerly
advanced by the Liberal party. Far from abandoning the "two-
nations" theory, he at the same time moved closer to the tradi-
tionalist sentiments still current in Quebec. His "option" thus
joined the traditional ideology of survival with the alleged prerequisite of political independence and economic autonomy. For those
whose expectations had been raised by the Quiet Revolution, but at
the same time remained embedded in their own culture, Lévesque's
proposals had a powerful appeal.

On June 3, 1968, representatives of the MSA, the RN, and the
RIN met to discuss a merger. The MSA now numbered over
10,000 members; in six months it had become the largest pro-
independence organization in Quebec's history. Its members
tended to be older than the RIN's adherents, chiefly male, middle
class, and professional or white collar. All might have proceeded
smoothly, but later that month a group of RIN members, in a last-
ditch show of support for unilingualism, occupied an English-
language public school. This, of course, ran counter to Lévesque's
insistence that the rights of Quebec's English-speaking minority be
protected. Then, on June 24, RIN militants participated in a riot
against Prime Minister Pierre Trudeau, charging him with being a
"traitor" and a "sellout." In five hours, 292 people were arrested.
Ninety-six policemen were injured and twelve cars damaged or

destroyed. Lévesque's response was to break off all negotiations. At that point little could have been more harmful than an identification, in the eyes of the public, with the RIN. By publicly disavowing their tactics he not only saved face; he also won the firm support of the RN.[20]

Lévesque was now in a position to set the terms for the organization of a new political party. These were, first, the creation of a French-language state in Quebec; second, the establishment of a democratic form of government; third, respect for the fundamental rights of individuals and minority groups, including the educational rights of the English-speaking minority in Quebec; and fourth, the negotiation of an economic association treaty, including a tariff and monetary union. On August 2, the RN accepted all four points. The RIN which had been invited to join the new organization, refused to accept the third point, and withdrew.

On October 11, 800 MSA and RN delegates met to found the Parti Québécois. René Lévesque was elected president, with Gilles Grégoire of the RN as vice-president. A party program, modeled on the MSA's, was adopted, again calling for the creation of a French-language republic, economic union with Canada, and the protection of minority rights. In addition, the PQ spelled out, for the first time, the means by which independence would be reached. This was to be a unilateral proclamation of independence, prior to negotiation with Ottawa. In the years preceding the party's 1976 electoral victory, and in the years that followed it as well, this policy would be progressively modified. An independent Quebec would, the program continued, assert its "inalienable rights" over its historical territories, including Labrador. Finally, the PQ pledged to establish a Bank of Quebec, thus altering Lévesque's earlier promise to negotiate an economic union with Canada.[21]

By October 1968 the PQ claimed 20,000 paid-up members. Among them were many who had become disillusioned with the RIN, which disbanded shortly after the PQ's founding congress. There was now a single, serious pro-independence party. It had, according to one observer, "all the stars." By incorporating the RN and a large number of former RIN members, it had moved toward the center politically and it stood ready to pose a serious threat to Quebec's two major parties. In April 1969, a poll published in the Montreal *Star* showed that the PQ was favored by 23 percent of its sample, as contrasted with 27 percent each for the Liberal party and the governing party, the Union Nationale. Significantly, its author, Peter Regenstreif, found that its supporters were more

often concerned with social and economic issues than with independence. A separate Quebec, they believed, would offer the social
and economic mobility they yearned for; there was also a strong
feeling that the working class would also benefit.

The PQ plunged into electoral politics in 1970. For the first time,
the question of independence was placed squarely before the voters. "We are—Québécois," read the campaign posters. "the time
has come to say: Yes. Yes, to normal liberty in friendship with
others. Yes, to normal security, and an end to prying. Yes, to
normal responsibility, which is the only true driving force for progress at every level, beginning with the economy. Yes, quite simply
to a normal life in a normal Quebec. Yes, on April 29, let's vote for
Quebec."[22] The PQ's program stressed social and economic issues—unemployment, education, the economy. Yet the underlying
issue, independence, was undeniable. In the week preceding the
election, Claude Ryan, the influential editor of *Le Devoir*, who
would later assume the leadership of the Quebec Liberal party in its
fight against the sovereignty-association referendum, reminded the
nation:

> The people of Quebec must first decide whether they will vote to
> break the federal link with the rest of Canada or to retain this link
> during the next four years. They may have a thousand different reasons
> for supporting the Parti Québécois. They should not forget that, in
> voting for this party, they are voting in favor of Quebec's political
> separation from the rest of Canada. . . .
> It is vital therefore that next Wednesday the people of Quebec state
> clearly whether they are for or against retaining the federal link as it
> now stands. Secondly, supposing they are in favor or retaining the
> federal link, they must say which of the three other parties is best suited
> to ensure the political development of Quebec within a Canadian
> framework.

Ryan concluded that the Liberals, under the leadership of Robert
Bourassa, were the "most capable of bringing about an economic
upsurge and at the same time the rationalization of public administration of which Quebec stands so much in need."[23]

When the results were in, the Liberals had won a clear majority
in the National Assembly; they now held 72 out of a total of 108
seats. The Union Nationale was reduced to 17, down from 56, and
the conservative Creditiste party had won 12. The Parti Québécois
had seven. But the percentage of the total vote received by each
party told a different story. The Liberals had won 41.8 percent of

the popular vote, as opposed to 47 percent in 1966; the Union Nationale was down to 19.6 percent from 41 percent; the Creditistes had won 11.1 percent. The Parti Québécois, in its first electoral campaign, had won 23 percent of the vote, this time drawing much of its support from the former supporters of the Union Nationale. Furthermore, the Liberals owed their victory to the solid support of the English-speaking community. In an interview published later that year, Lévesque charged that 95 percent of this group had voted Liberal. "Even little old ladies on stretchers were hauled out in the end-of-regime panic, as if it were the end of the Roman Empire." Without the organized opposition of the English-speaking community, he asserted, the number of PQ seats would have been substantially higher.[24]

The period between the elections of 1970 and 1973 was a time of crisis and retrenchment for the independence movement. The October crisis of 1970 had tarnished its image and reduced its appeal; many Quebecers were unwilling to admit publicly that they supported independence. By September 1971, the PQ's membership had fallen from 80,000 to 35,000.[25] In addition, friction between the party's moderate and left wings had weakened it internally. Lévesque, always mindful of public opinion, was reluctant to lend PQ support to public demonstrations which he feared might result in violence. In an effort to clarify its goals, the party therefore prepared a manifesto, *Quand nous serons vraiment chez nous,*[26] which it distributed to its members in 1972. It was published in book format the following year. In it the PQ rejected both "doctrinaire socialism" and "grandfather capitalism, pledging to create a social democracy based on Quebec's vast economic and human resources, a more equitable division of wealth and an opportunity to participate, for the first time in history, in the determination of their collective interests.

In an eloquent and evocative introduction, *Quand nous serons vraiment chez nous* argued that this new society could be achieved only through independence. It began with a lengthy quotation the MSA's 1967 manifesto. "We are Quebecers," it declared.

> What that means . . . is that we are attached to the only corner of the world where we can be fully ourselves, this Quebec which, we are well aware, is the only place where it is possible to be truly at home.
>
> To be ourselves is essentially to maintain and develop a personality which has lasted three and a half centuries. At the heart of this personality is the fact that we speak French. Everything else is tied to this essential element or inevitably leads back to it.[27]

Quebecers were the heirs to that "fantastic adventure" which had created a North America almost entirely French and of an obstinacy that had made possible the survival of its last fragment, Quebec. This fact, this "vital difference," distinguished them from all other North Americans. In the past Quebec's "personality" had survived because of its isolation. Now, however, its very existence was threatened. A society that considers itself inferior will eventually be unable to accept itself, the manifesto declared. Its minority position on an Anglo-Saxon continent posed a constant temptation to reject itself in order to conform with the majority. For this reason it was essential that Quebec seize the opportunity to take control of its own destiny. This option would not last forever; the forces of assimilation were already at work.[28]

By September 25, when Premier Robert Bourassa called for new elections, *Quand nous serons vraiment chez nous* had been widely circulated. The party convention, held in Montreal in February of that year, had adopted a program which softened, to some extent, the radical proposals of the earlier publication. Yet despite Lévesque's efforts to allay the fears of Quebec's voters, the election was seen as a choice for or against independence. Those who voted for the PQ were, for a variety of reasons, strongly committed to its goals; those who voted Liberal were less intensely committed to their choice, but regarded the possible economic problems of a newly independent Quebec as a serious threat.[29] The 1976 election would witness a shift of many of these voters to the Parti Québécois.

By polarizing the electorate on the independence issue, the Parti Québécois radically altered the party system that had lasted nearly forty years. Its entry into electoral politics in 1970, along with the Créditistes, had created a multiparty system, with the PQ holding the balance; by 1973, its vigorous campaign on the independence issue had displaced the Union Nationale as the second major party. The election of October 29 returned the Liberals to power with 54.8 percent of the vote, up from 41.8 percent three years earlier, and with an overwhelming majority of seats in the National Assembly, 102 out of 110.[30] Most of their strength, however, was drawn not from their ideological opponent, the Party Québécois, but from the Union Nationale, whose support dropped from 19.6 to a mere 4.9 percent of the votes cast, losing all of its 17 seats. The most significant change was in the strength of the Parti Québécois, which, while losing one of its seats, now commanded 30.3 percent of the vote, up from 23 percent in the last election.[31]

The returns of the 1973 election made the PQ all the more aware of the need to broaden its appeal. To Claude Morin, a former deputy minister of intergovernmental affairs and since 1972 a member of the PQ, this meant softening the party's stand on independence. The issue of a referendum, raised during the campaign but never fully explained, became the subject of renewed discussion the following spring. Morin insisted upon a referendum as an absolute requirement before any declaration of independence could be made. Despite opposition within the party, Lévesque agreed with Morin, and this view prevailed. In October 1975 the Executive Council and the Parliamentary wing passed a resolution stating that "a period of transition is inevitable—even if Ottawa agrees— there would be delays for such matters as beginning negotiations, etc."[32] The Parti Québécois thus affirmed that independence would not quickly follow electoral victory. By breaking the situation which had confronted the voters with an either/or proposition, the PQ had made itself more squarely competitive with the Liberal party. In addition, it now gave the people of Quebec a double option—of voting first for the freedom to choose independence, and later for independence itself.

The Parti Québécois's 1976 program, formulated at the party congress earlier that year, included lengthy social, economic, and cultural proposals. In a sharp contrast with earlier publications, the party's commitment to independence was introduced not as a policy to be implemented, but as an "historic objective" to be considered. Independence, the program urged, "need not and should not result in a complete break with Canada. The economy of the two would remain complementary, and it would be in their mutual interest to maintain existing commercial ties such as those linking Ontario and Quebec. The institution of French as the official language, also a central policy of the Parti Québécois, was presented as part of its cultural policy; however, the PQ pledged to protect the rights of English-speaking and other ethnic minorities. Finally, the means of achieving independence was spelled out. After stressing the need for a better electoral system, increased aid to municipalities, reforms in public administration, a legal-aid system, prison reform, and the political rights of native peoples, the program turned at last to the issue of independence. "This can only be decided democratically with the support of the population," it declared. The means of arriving at this decision were left somewhat ambiguous. The PQ promised to "adopt a general law on referendums which will guarantee that the options available to the people are clearly understood so that they will be able to express their true choices." In addition, the PQ promised to "integrate into the new civil service (without loss of financial benefits to the employees concerned) all Quebec residents currently working for the Federal government who wish to be 'repatriated.'" Finally, the party promised to "participate fully in international life, while keeping close ties with Canada and the United States and seeking close collaboration with Francophone nations." The program pledged a pacifist policy which "could substantially reduce military expenses, by replacing the traditional armed forces with territorial defence units." This policy would allow the government to save vast sums of money, which could then be used for the economic, social, and cultural development of Quebec.[33]

This was the program with which the PQ entered the electoral campaign of 1976. The independence issue had been softened to the point where it no longer posed a threat to a decisive minority of Quebecers. Since the last election other issues had arisen, producing what Pinard and Hamilton have called an "increasing gap" between support for independence itself and support for its main organ, the Parti Québécois. To some extent this was the result of the party's 1975 decision to disassociate electoral victory from independence.

In July 1976 Lévesque outlined a possible scenario in *Foreign Affairs:* "Let us suppose it does happen, and Quebec peacefully elects such a government. What then?" At the very least, Lévesque said, Quebec would try to negotiate with Canada. But first, "there would have to be the referendum which the Parti Québécois proposed in order to get the decisive yes-or-no answer to the tired question: what *does* Quebec want?" Reminding his readers that Newfoundland had used this device as a means of determining whether to join the Confederation, he suggested that a referendum was an equally appropriate means for opting out. If the referendum results were negative, he added, "then there's nothing to do but wait for the momentum of change to keep on working until the answer is yes."[34]

If the change in Lévesque's rhetoric was reassuring, political forces in Quebec also played a crucial role in increasing support for the Parti Québécois. The Liberal government had been plagued by a number of problems, including cost overruns on the James Bay Hydroelectric installations and the 1976 Olympics, which took place in Montreal. High unemployment and tense labor relations were blamed on the Liberals. In addition, a number of labor contracts in the public sector were to be renegotiated that year. A number of work stoppages occurred; the worst was a five-week nurses' strike. Finally, the Liberal government's attempts to improve the status of the French language in Quebec had resulted in a situation that antagonized Anglophones and Francophones alike. Bill 22, the government's response to the failures of bilingualism, made French the official language of Quebec and required its use in government. In addition, it provided for the gradual implementation of the French language in business, and it mandated French as the language of instruction in the public schools. While English-language instruction was provided for the children of English-speaking parents, those who could not pass a proficiency test were required to enroll in French schools. Italian, Greek, Portuguese, and Chinese immigrants, enraged at what they considered a violation of their right to choose freely between the two cultures, withdrew their support of the Liberal party.[35]

The 1976 election took place at a time when federal-provincial relations, which had been strained for years, were entering into a critical phase. The issue revolved around Prime Minister Trudeau's efforts to repatriate the British North America Act. A constitutional conference, held in June 1971, had ended abruptly when Quebec's delegation rejected the proposed Victoria Charter. The failure of the conference had led to an increasing resistance throughout Canada to Trudeau's policy of bilingualism, and to an increasing demand within Quebec that the present Constitution be drastically revised, if not replaced, so as to offer a new form of association guaranteeing Quebec control over internal matters, and making formal provision for the distinctly different style of relations with Ottawa which, in the view of many observers, already existed.[36] It was on this issue, in 1976, that Premier Bourassa requested a mandate. In calling for a new election, he emphasized the coming discussions of Quebec's status with its "Canadian partners." These discussions, he said, were "the most important in a long time for our future. In order to associate all Quebecers with this historical decision-making process which will result in the birth of a new Canada, I have decided to hold a general election November 15." Bourassa's program included a proposal for a new constitution including, among other things, Quebec's right to exclude itself from any federal program with fiscal compensation, control over immigration, and the power to veto unilaterally any future amendments to the constitution. His expressed hope was to unify Quebecers behind a set of concrete proposals that would strengthen his bargaining position with the federal government.[37]

In presenting his case to the people, Bourassa portrayed the choice as one between a special status and separation. In the closing weeks of the campaign large posters with the caption, "Stop separatism! Bourassa—only he can do it! Vote Liberal" appeared. If the PQ had been running chiefly on the independence issue, as it had in 1973, the Liberals might have succeeded. But in 1976 the PQ was in fact running on a variety of issues, consisting of a "a set of very negative evaluations of the Liberal government, as well as a set of positive evaluations of the PQ party, its leadership and its platform on issues other than independence." By requiring a referendum, it had made certain that independence was no longer an immediate issue for many voters. Interestingly enough, the PQ's posters, rather than joining issue with the Liberals' attack on "separatism," focused on the Liberals themselves. "This can't continue," posters blared, in a reference to evidence of widespread corruption within the Liberal government. "Enough is enough," the party's English-language brochure pleaded.[38]

Even before the campaign was over, a poll conducted by Pinard and Hamilton showed the PQ leading the liberals 50 to 27 percent. Yet there were few who were not stunned by the PQ victory. The party had increased in strength in every district; it had won 41.4 percent of the popular vote and 71 seats in the National Assembly. Throughout Canada politicans and journalists tried to deny the significance of what had just happened. Nevertheless, Quebec had taken her first giant step in the direction of independence. "For the first time," writes Saywell, "it was clear that independence was regarded as one of the rational and legitimate options open to the Québécois. Neither the province nor the country could ever be quite the same again."[39]

The dramatic shifts which occurred within the Quebec electorate in the three provincial elections of the 1970s may be attributed to several factors. Certainly the introduction of the independence issue and the entry of the PQ into electoral politics were responsible for the decline of the Union Nationale. David Butler and Donald Stokes identify three basic conditions which must be met if a political issue is to affect the results of an election: a "bond of issue to self," a "strong trend of opinion" in one direction or another, and a perception of party policies and capabilities with respect to the issue.[40] Although the majority of voters in the three elections held during the decade favored a continuation of the federal system, an increasing number believed that some form of independence was desirable. In addition, the three major parties, the Liberals, the Union Nationale, and the PQ, presented the voters with relatively clear alternatives.

In 1976, however, the issues were less clear cut. Although the Parti Québécois was able to retain the support of those who had voted for it in the two earlier elections, the independence issue was no longer an immediate one and was now competing with a series of other issues, despite the Liberals' unsuccessful attempts to identify the independence issue as the salient one. John Meisel has noted that even within Quebec, cleavages in religion and language do not extend to party affiliation.[41] This would help to explain the willingness of voters to cross party lines when they perceived that the issues involved warranted it.[42]

There is, in addition, the "issue" of "majority" government. LeDuc notes a strong preference for majority government within Canada as a whole, and a tendency on the part of the electorate to cross party lines in order to avoid minority governments such as Trudeau's in 1972–74. A "slight regional pattern appears in 1974 with favourable attitudes toward majority government being highest in Quebec and lowest in the West."[43] While these observations refer to national elections, it is worth noting that, despite the entry of the PQ and other minority parties, Quebecers elected a clear parliamentary majority in each of the provincial elections of the 1970s. Furthermore, each of the elections clearly identified an unofficial opposition party within the Quebec legislature. In "The Role of Opposition in a One-Party Dominant System: The Case of Ontario," LeDuc and Walter H. White argue that one-party dominance "would seem to be not the exception, but the rule, in provincial political systems," and that the role of the opposition party is determined by the nature of the system.[44] Given the tendency of political parties within Quebec to fall into the roles of majority party and an opposition party, it is not surprising that with the emergence of the independence issue these realignments occurred.

Once in office, Lévesque directed his efforts toward establishing the credibility of his government and broadening its popular support. The question of a referendum was naturally paramount in most people's minds. Lévesque made it clear that it would not be immediately forthcoming. He was well aware that the party had not won on the independence issue, and that it had been elected by less than a majority. At the First Ministers Conference on December 13, he emphasized, "I do not wish to repeat it, that we do not claim to see this vote as a mandate for Quebec's independence. Our commitments are clear on this point: when the time comes it will be up to the public and to them alone to decide the issue in a referendum." His first task, he added, would be to win the support of Quebec's voters.[45]

But within months of the election Lévesque and his party began to lay the groundwork for the referendum. The official program of the Parti Québécois, adopted at the party's sixth National Convention in May 1977, promised a referendum "during its first mandate," or term of office, "at the time it judges most opportune," followed by the patriation of those powers entrusted to Ottawa under the existing constitutional arrangements, and discussions with the federal government leading to the transfer of these powers and the division of debits and credits. A system of government, essentially the American presidential format, was outlined, and provisions made for the protection of the rights of native peoples. But what stood out most sharply, in contrast with the party's 1976 program, was the statement of general policy:

> Four centuries of common history have formed French Quebecers into a nation, which has always contained in its bosom a large minority of people from a variety of backgrounds, whose basic rights it has respected more than most other nations. This founding people has always manifested the desire to develop its own distinctive culture. But it has become obvious, with time, that this objective can only be achieved if it has full control over the reins of its political life.
>
> Quebec desperately needs a prosperous, dynamic economy to ensure the long-term survival of its French culture. Time and again federalism has proven to work against the best interests of Quebec's majority. This is an intolerable situation. No collectivity can indefinitely entrust its destiny to others without losing its dignity and severely compromising its survival.
>
> Although Quebec has all of the material and human resources to attain political sovereignty, it cannot live in isolation—any more than any other people. Conscious of the ties of interdependence that bind the various nations together, it is ready to take its place among them as a responsible, dynamic partner, especially in view of the privileged links created by geography and history.[46]

As the primary architect of his party's strategy, Lévesque faced the double pressure of making good his promise to hold a referendum during his first term of office and winning confidence in the proposal for sovereignty-association fast enough to maintain the credibility of his government. If the PQ was to remain in power, and indeed, if it hoped to show any strength in its negotiations with Canada, it was necessary to have some evidence that the 1976 election represented more than a superficial expression of dissatisfaction with the Bourassa regime. Slowly, the emphasis on independence gave way to an emphasis on sovereignty. This stance was softened still further when Claude Morin, Quebec's Minister of Intergovernmental Affairs, announced at the conclusion of a three-day visit to London that a sovereign Quebec would remain in the Commonwealth.

On June 3, 1978, the long-awaited referendum bill was passed by the National Assembly. The new law required that the legislature debate and pass, by a simple majority, the proposition that the government planned to submit to the people. A campaign period of at least thirty days would follow, after which the public would vote on the proposal. Ballots would be printed in French and English and, where necessary, in Indian and Eskimo languages. The results would not be legally binding; however, the Lévesque government declared that it would consider itself morally bound by the results. It added that the referendum would take place some time in 1979.[47] Perhaps the most interesting feature of this legislation was the government's assertion that it would consider itself morally bound by any referendum it organized. Presumably, a vote against independence would incur a commitment on the part of the PQ not to seek independence in the immediate future.

In September 1978, Prime Minister Trudeau announced that federal elections would be held the following spring. Shortly afterward, Lévesque declared that the referendum would be delayed at least until the fall of that year, in order to allow time for an "extensive national debate" on the independence issue. By now he had reason to believe that time was on his side. A poll published that month showed 53.4 percent of its sample satisfied with the government, up from 46 percent in June. More significantly, 38 percent indicated that they would vote for sovereignty-association, while 36 percent said they would vote against it. Despite the large number (25 percent) who expressed no opinion, those who supported Lévesque's plan were now in the lead.

That same month, Ottawa agreed to renew discussion of the federal-provincial division of power. In October a three-day constitutional conference opened in Ottawa. As an elected government, the PQ sent representatives, stating that it would seek increased powers under the present arrangements. But Lévesque made it clear that he still planned to seek a new partnership, based on sovereignty-association, following the referendum. The conference ended inconclusively with the agreement to set up a ministerial-level committee to continue discussions. Trudeau had been unable to get the provincial ministers to agree on a revision of the division of powers between the federal and provincial governments, and Lévesque, in particular, had insisted that there was no possibility of his government's accepting patriation without a firm guarantee that Quebec would have "all powers necessary to ensure its own development."

By early 1979, Quebec still maintained its commitment to sovereignty. Yet as never before, Quebec's ministers were preparing to work within the existing framework until such time as that autonomy became a reality. At a meeting of First Ministers in January, Claude Morin announced that Quebec's policy had remained consistent over most of this century. "Quebec has always wanted greater provincial autonomy," he said, adding that Quebec would, for the time being, work within the present constitutional system. At the same time, René Lévesque was portraying an independent Quebec in terms that would have been unrecognizable to the old RIN members. "Quebec," he asserted, would remain a small but staunch partner of English-speaking Canada and the United States when independence comes. Quebec would maintain "its old links of friendship with the United States and would participate actively in the security arrangements of the Atlantic Alliance, as a member of NORAD and NATO."[48]

In January, a federal task force released its report on Canadian unity. Headed by Jean-Luc Pépin, a former federal cabinet minister, and John Robarts, a former prime minister of Ontario, it began with the recommendation that all provinces should have responsibility for protecting their linguistic minorities. Quebec, the report stated, should not be required to provide more protection for its English-speaking citizens than the English Canadian provinces currently do for their French-speaking minorities. Then came the bombshell: "The task Force believes that the progressive extension of the majority language in Quebec is inevitable and those provisions of Article 133 on the use of English in Quebec of the B.N.A.A. incompatible with the aspirations of the Quebec people should be abrogated." In addition, the report recommended that the unenumerated powers in the constitution be attributed to the provinces, rather than to the federal government, and that fiscal compensation be offered to provinces that opted out of federal programs.

In an interview on the *McNeil-Lehrer Report*, Lévesque expressed doubts that English Canada would accept the Pepin-Robarts report, and he predicted that the rejection of its recommendations would increase the appeal of independence. Less than two weeks later, a Gallup poll revealed that 46 percent of Quebecers would now vote in favor of a sovereignty-association if accompanied by an economic union with Canada. Only 39 percent were opposed; the portion of those undecided had dropped to 15 percent.

Then on February 12, a week-long constitutional conference ended. It had ignored both the Pepin-Robarts report and, for the most part, the coming to power of the Parti Québécois. Even the relatively moderate demands of the Liberals were overlooked. Shortly afterward, Lévesque announced that his government would not participate in any further constitutional conferences until after the referendum. The anticipated federal elections—which were later called for May 22—would be followed by pre-referendum and referendum period debates. It was, he said, impossible to continue negotiations with Ottawa and the other provinces at the same time as the referendum. The referendum would give Quebec a bargaining power that it had not previously had. This admission may well underscore the ambiguous status of the PQ: to remain in power it must define its position in terms that distinguish it very little from the governing party it displaced, the Liberal party. Thus the referendum was presented not only as a choice for independence but as a means of increasing the PQ's bargaining power in a revision of the federal system, an ingenious appeal to both sides.

In March, a CBC survey found 51 percent of Quebecers in favor of granting "a mandate to negotiate sovereignty association" to the Lévesque administration, the highest affirmative response to that date. The poll also showed an increasing support outside Quebec, an indication that the bargaining might be less difficult than at an earlier date.

The election of May 22, 1979, brought the Conservative party under Joe Clark to power after eleven years of Liberal rule. It also brought to a temporary halt Trudeau's efforts to preserve Canada as a bi-cultural society. The vote was polarized along linguistic lines. Although the Liberals received overwhelming support in Quebec, the Conservatives won easily in Ontario and the western

provinces. Clark's cabinet, chosen from among the elected representatives of his own party (as is the rule in parliamentary systems),
included only two French Canadians. The results, Lévesque said,
showed that two nations existed. Scarcely a month later, on June
21, Lévesque announced that Quebec voters would be asked to
participate in a referendum on sovereignty association in the spring
of 1980. Lévesque called the referendum a historic choice, one that
should be made in an unpressured atmosphere. In the same speech
he also noted that the new federal government would present its
constitutional proposal "in the next few months," and that the
provincial Liberals would offer their own views of federalism in the
fall. "I do not feel we should try to take a head start on the others,"
he said. "All sides must have the opportunity to put all their cards
face-up on the table. Everyone must get involved."[49]

On November 2, 1979, the Lévesque government issued its
white paper on sovereignty-association, *Quebec-Canada: A New Deal*.
Reviewing the history of Quebec up through the most recent
efforts to deal with the problem of Canadian dualism, it argued that
all attempts to resolve the conflict between the "two majorities"—
the French-speaking majority within Quebec and the English-
speaking majority within Canada—had reached an impasse. This
deadlock had been recognized fifteen years earlier in the Lauren-
deau-Dunton report. Yet the question remained: How can this
equality be reconciled within a ten-province federation? Breaking
the deadlock, the report argued, would mean that

> we will have to resign ourselves to giving up to the central government,
> in which Quebecers will always be a minority, an impressive number of
> prerogatives and decision-making centres that to date Quebec has been
> demanding for itself.
>
> For Quebecers that would mean implicitly accepting the fact that
> control over some of their most vital affairs would go to a government
> over which they could never exert more than an indirect or passing
> influence; it would mean entrusting their interests and their future to
> others. Very few nations in the world would be satisfied with such an
> arrangement.[50]

The only way out of this deadlock, the white paper concluded,
was to admit the impossibility of renewed federalism, and to choose
instead a formula which would "satisfy both Quebec's needs for
autonomy and the equally normal need of English Canada for cohesion."[51]

The "New Deal" proposed by the Quebec government began

with a listing of both actual associations and forms of association for sovereign states, described several general formulas for integration—the free-trade zone, the customs union, the common market, and the monetary union—and called first for a monetary association between the two communities. "Replacing federalism by association [would] maintain economic exchange, but the nature of political and legal relations between Quebec and Canada [would] be changed." Sovereignty, the basis for negotiating these changes, implied "the power to levy all taxes, to make all laws, and to be present on the international scene"; it was, in addition, the power "to share freely, with one or more states, certain national powers." The existing rights of the Anglophone minority under the current federal arrangements would be continued, and rights of the Amerindian and Inuit communities were guaranteed.

Although the Quebec courts would be the only judicial system, a joint court would be created to deal with cases arising under the treaty to be negotiated between Quebec and Canada.

As for external relations, Quebec pledged to "continue to be bound by existing treaties," although the document reserved the right to withdraw in the future where permitted by international law. As promised earlier, Quebec would remain a partner in NATO and NORAD and would seek admission to the United Nations. Although relations with other Francophone countries would be developed, Quebec promised to consider remaining within the British Commonwealth.[52]

The nature of the association to be formed was less defined. Its guiding principle was to be the legal equality of the partners. Although it was expected that Canada would be represented by the central government, there would be no objection to certain provinces being "parties on the Canadian side of the association," thus admitting the possibility of future changes within the Canadian federation. The free circulation of goods, a monetary union, and the free circulation of peoples were identified as areas of common action; areas of common interest included matters such as transportation, regulation of labor, and the balance of payments.

Finally, there were to be four community agencies, a community council, a commission of experts, a court of justice, and a monetary authority to deal with matters such as the money supply, the rate of exchange, and distribution of the public debt and government revenues.[53]

Despite the relatively specific proposals of the White Paper, the referendum question, introduced in Quebec's National Assembly

on December 20 and formally approved the following March, did
not ask the voters to agree to sovereignty-association, but only to
authorize their government "to negotiate a new agreement with
Canada." It was, in the words of Pinard and Hamilton, "a 'soft'
question, made even softer by the promise of a second referendum
before any change could be effected as a result of negotiations."[54]
The question read:

> The Government of Quebec has made public its proposal to
> negotiate a new agreement with the rest of Canada, based on the equal-
> ity of nations;
>   this agreement would enable Quebec to acquire the exclusive power
> to make its laws, levy its taxes and establish relations abroad—in other
> words, sovereignty—and at the same time, to maintain with Canada an
> economic association including a common currency;
>   no change in political status resulting from these negotiations will be
> effected without approval by the people through another referendum;
>   on these terms, do you give the Government of Quebec the mandate
> to negotiate the proposed agreement between Quebec and Canada?[55]

Reportedly drafted by Daniel Latouche, a political scientist at
McGill University on leave since 1978 as Adviser on Canadian and
Constitutional Affairs, the referendum question epitomized
Lévesque's *étapiste* (after the French word for step) strategy: the
mandate expressed in the 1976 election was to be followed by a
more specific mandate to negotiate, followed by a further mandate
before any agreed-upon changes could be put into effect. Lévesque
would later add an extra half-step to this strategy by urging even
those who opposed separation to vote *oui* as a means of strengthening Quebec's position in future federal-provincial negotiations, thus
increasing his chances that the referendum would pass (although
lessening the significance of the *oui* vote) and buying time to persuade such voters to support his position in a final referendum.

The Liberal party countered with its alternative to sovereignty-
association, *A New Canadian Federation*, released on January 9,
1980. Based on the working paper, *To Choose Quebec and Canada*,
which Claude Ryan had produced a year earlier, this document,
popularly called the Beige Paper after the color of its cover, offered
an extensive plan for revising the Canadian federation.

The Beige Paper began with an acknowledgment of the
seriousness of the choice that lay ahead. It identified as the chief
objective of the Parti Québécois and the Quebec government the
proposal "to make Quebec a fully sovereign state." A *oui* vote in the

coming referendum was "synonymous with sovereignty, with independence, and with political separation from the rest of Canada." As for the "association" portion of the deal, the Beige Paper went on to declare that, in view of "the uniformly negative response of the other provinces to the publication of the White Paper . . . The Parti Québécois' plan for economic association is truly a 'house of cards.' "[56]

The pessimism over the collective future of Quebec and Canada was, according to the Beige Paper, unwarranted. The Liberal option to remain within the Canadian federation was based on the confidence that the federal framework provided the best possibilities for Quebec "to develop freely, in accordance with its own nature, and at the same time to participate, without renouncing its own identity, in the benefits and challenges of a larger and much richer society." This could be achieved only through constitutional reform.[57]

The basis for such reform was the principle of Canadian cultural dualism and the need to preserve the right of the two "founding peoples." This was to be guaranteed through a series of provisions, including a veto power over amendments to certain clauses in the Canadian constitution, alternating appointment from Quebec and the English-speaking provinces of the Chief Justice of the Supreme Court, together with a requirement that on constitutional issues four of the remaining eight justices be from Quebec.

The principle of duality in cultural matters would be guaranteed by a committee composed equally of Anglophones and Francophones whose ratification would be required on all acts of Parliament dealing with linguistic and cultural matters, and by a Federal Council with sweeping powers over "all central government proposals affecting the fundamental equilibrium of the federation," most senior-level appointments, and treaties affecting provincial affairs. In addition, it was to possess advisory powers on a far broader range of issues. Twenty-five percent of the council would be from Quebec, a proportion not subject to change despite the decreasing population. A two-thirds majority would be necessary for ratification. This would have meant that Quebec, holding a quarter of the vote, could, by means of an alliance with just over eight percent of the membership, paralyze the entire central government on any number of issues, a power far greater than that held by an upper house such as the United States Senate, and even greater in view of the fact that the smaller provinces would have been over-represented in this scheme.

Other provisions included a constitutionally enshrined charter of rights and liberties, the institutionalization of the federal-provincial conference as a mechanism for constitutional reform, and adoption of any new constitution by a two-step process consisting of approval by provincial legislatures and ratification by the electorate, and, in order to ensure legal continuity, renunciation by the British Parliament of its right to alter Canada's Constitution.[58]

Finally, the Beige Paper offered its proposals for an amending formula which, while permitting greater flexibility than the laws currently in force, was so conceived as "to prevent unilateral amendment of basic elements of the Constitution by a simple majority vote."[59]

The Beige Paper can be understood both as a reaction to sovereignty and as an attempt to formulate, at the eleventh hour, a set of proposals which would persuade Quebecers to give federalism one more chance. In both respects, it served its purpose. Yet despite its elaborate presentation and profusion of suggestions, the Liberal party's program was simply not capable of being implemented. Although a majority of Quebecers thought enough of the Beige Paper's proposals to vote *non* in the referendum, to English Canada the proposals were simply unacceptable. Yet, as Jane Jacobs observes in *The Question of Separatism*, "English Canada found itself in the position of relying upon these proposals and their chief proponent, Ryan, as a means of defeating separatist sentiment."[60]

Then on February 18, 1980, federal elections returned the Liberal party, with Pierre Trudeau once again at the helm, to power. During less than nine months, the Progressive Conservatives' working majority had shrunk to a single vote, and the government finally succumbed to the combined pressures of energy pricing and the declining value of the Canadian dollar. Although Prime Minister Clark had declined to involve himself in the referendum, claiming that it was a provincial issue, Trudeau campaigned on a promise to defend Canadian federalism. Once in office, he offered renewed hope to those who believed in the capabilities of Canada's federal system to provide a solution to the problem of Quebec's status and who thought that constitutional reform could be achieved through one more try at federal-provincial negotiation. Although Trudeau actually involved himself very little until the final stages of the campaign, on May 11 he promised that if the *non* won, he would move without delay for a federal-provincial conference on patriating the constitution.

The defeat of the referendum on May 20, 1980, was hailed throughout Canada as a definitive choice, in which Quebecers had firmly declared their allegiance to Canada and their rejection of Separatism. As the votes were being counted Trudeau declared, "Now that we have reaffirmed our will to live together, we must apply ourselves without delay to the task of rebuilding our home to conform to the present needs of the Canadian family." The following day, Trudeau announced that efforts to rework Canada's constitution would begin at once. "We Canadians," he told the House of Commons, "are now agreed on a common destination. What we must now do is chart a new course toward that destination."

Despite the magnitude of the *non* vote—the referendum was defeated 59.6 percent to 40.4 percent or by a vote of 2,187,991 to 1,485,761—and despite pre-referendum claims by both sides that this was to be a historic choice, the results actually determined very little as far as Quebec's status was concerned. Had the referendum won, Lévesque would have been in the position of initiating negotiations with Canada. The wording of the referendum question, the opposition of the English-speaking provinces, Trudeau's refusal to negotiate, and the fact that new provincial elections would have to be held within eighteen months made it doubtful that any significant change could have been accomplished within the near future. Armed with a *oui* vote but facing a political impasse, Lévesque might well have found himself in an untenable position.

But the *non* vote was just as inconclusive. When, on referendum night it became clear that the *non* had won, Lévesque conceded that "the people of Quebec have clearly given federalism another chance." But, he warned, "The ball is now in the Federalist court. Within the next weeks and months they will be called upon to prove that they can redeem their pledge to create a renewed federation."

Having lost the referendum but not an election, Lévesque was in a peculiar position. He would soon have to represent his province at constitutional talks, yet by his own admission Quebec's position was far weaker than it would have been if the referendum had won. He had claimed that Quebec's demands for equality could not be met within the existing ten-province federation, but he was now in the position of having to negotiate a constitutional arrangement that would be acceptable both to the people of Quebec and to the Parti Québécois. He also had to deal with the Liberals' call for new elections, routine in most parliamentary systems. But for Lévesque, rejection of the referendum, though it hurt "more than any electoral defeat," was not to be equated with rejection of his government. Despite Ryan's claim that as a proponent of sovereignty-association, Lévesque had no plan for constitutional change within the existing system, Lévesque promised to negotiate in good faith and to cooperate with Canada in pursuit of an acceptable solution.

The promise of a renewed federalism proved to be illusory, at least for Quebec. During the summer of 1980 the ten premiers tried in vain to agree on a set of preliminary principles for constitutional change. At issue were the distribution of power between the federal government and the provinces and a charter of basic rights and freedoms that would further extend the powers of the central government by taking final authority on such matters away from the provincial legislatures and granting it to federally appointed judges. The question of an amending formula, less crucial for the other provinces, was deemed critical by Quebec: traditionally, the unanimity rule requiring consent of all ten provinces to any change in the British North America Act had provided Quebec with a virtual veto power over any attempts to erode her constitutional status. At the same time, Quebec's unwillingness to relinquish this power in subsequent constitutional arrangements, and the insistence by the nine other provinces on a new amendment-veto formula, had foiled all previous attempts at constitutional revision. In addition, there was the question of patriation: without an agreed-upon amending formula, Canada would have no means of changing the constitution. Until agreement could be reached, Canada would remain the only nation in the world with the dubious distinction of having to petition the parliament of another country for permission to change its own constitution.

With the issue of independence fading, Lévesque needed a new strategy for strengthening his position in negotiation. He could no longer hope to ensure Quebec's autonomy, either through sovereignty-association or through the implicit threat to Canadian unity which a solid *oui* vote might have presented. No longer strong enough to maintain a stance of opposition in the three-way confrontation between Quebec, the other provinces and the central government, Lévesque chose instead a strategy of accommodation. This strategy, in which Quebec joined with seven other provinces— Alberta, British Columbia, Manitoba, Newfoundland, Nova Scotia, Prince Edward Island, and Saskatchewan—would provoke a constitutional crisis before leading to the agreement by the nine

English-speaking provinces on a new constitution, and the isolation of Quebec in a position that by now had become traditional.

In seeking a strategy of accommodation, Lévesque was guided by Claude Morin, Minister of Intergovernmental Affairs. It was Morin's view that the first aim in any constitutional negotiations should be to "keep the options open"; a second obligation was to "conserve all the current powers of the Assemblée Nationale du Québec, Quebec's most powerful political tool." Specifically, that meant that Quebec, together with the other provinces, should oppose any attempt by Ottawa to increase its areas of jurisdiction at the expense of the provinces.[61]

During the annual premiers' conference in August 1980, word of a secret federal plan to patriate the Canadian constitution without provincial consent was leaked to an Ottawa newspaper. Trudeau had warned earlier that he would call upon the British Parliament to approve unilaterally a constitutional package in the event that no agreement was reached by September. The secret memo suggested convening the House of Commons and Senate earlier than scheduled for the purpose of debating and approving a resolution requesting Parliament to do so.

The 1980 constitutional conference, held in Ottawa from September 8 through 12, failed to produce agreement on any point. On September 18 the Trudeau government announced that it had agreed on a set of principles for a resolution on the constitution. In the weeks that followed, provincial opposition mounted to a crescendo while the House of Commons debated Trudeau's proposal. Lawsuits challenging the constitutionality of the plan were begun in Manitoba, Newfoundland, and Quebec. The growing opposition of the western provinces, however, was based not only on constitutional principle but also on Trudeau's attempt to expand the role of the federal government in economic matters. On this there was room for negotiation.

In February 1981, Manitoba's Court of Appeals determined that the federal plan was legal; the following month, Newfoundland's Court of Appeals held unanimously that it was illegal, and in April Quebec's highest court, in a 4-to-1 ruling, found it legal. The matter was immediately appealed to Canada's Supreme Court, which, on September 28, ruled that, although the federal government was not required as a matter of law to obtain consent of the provinces before seeking amendment by Parliament, their consent was required as a matter of constitutional convention. The ruling that the move was legal but not constitutional was interpreted by each side in the dispute to justify its own position. Jean Chrétien, Trudeau's Minister of Justice, announced that since a tradition did not equal law, the federal government could go ahead with its plan; but in the face of renewed opposition from the provinces and from the opposition in the House of Commons, Trudeau decided to give the premiers one final chance.

The ten premiers convened in Ottawa on November 2. The eight dissenting premiers were firm in their opposition to the charter of human rights. However, Lévesque, in a technical maneuver, had agreed to give up Quebec's traditional veto on constitutional change in an effort to forge an agreement on an amending formula. As part of the compromise, the provinces would be permitted to opt out of any future constitutional amendments that affected provincial rights. Lévesque was equally adamant about both the charter and the amending formula; events would soon prove that the other provinces were not. Faced with the alternative of having a constitution imposed on them, they agreed on a modified charter in return for keeping their amending formula. On November 5, 1981, the premiers of Canada's nine English-speaking provinces signed a new constitution in both English and French. Lévesque did not.

Since Lévesque had broken the traditional unanimity rule by his compromise on the amending formula, both Ottawa and the nine other provinces rejected his attempt to veto the new constitution. The motion requesting that "the Queens' Most Excellent Majesty . . . graciously be pleased to cause to be laid before the Parliament of the United Kingdom a measure containing the recitals and clauses hereinafter set forth," was formally approved on December 2, 1981, by Canada's House of Commons.

By 1982, the dream of a sovereign Quebec seemed more remote than at any time since the 1976 election. On April 17, in Ottawa, Queen Elizabeth II formally proclaimed the Constitution Act of 1982, thus completing the process of patriation. Although its ties with the British Parliament were now severed, Canada remained a constitutional monarchy with a British sovereign as its Queen. Relations between Quebec and English-speaking Canada remained tense. Both the Parti Québécois and many of the Quebec Liberals, including Claude Ryan, found the accord on the Constitution objectionable. René Lévesque was still seeking to have the deal invalidated by the federal courts, citing Quebec's traditional right to veto constitutional change; Trudeau maintained that the decision by the Supreme Court of Canada meant that Quebec's approval was not required.

Within Quebec, the mandate of the Parti Québécois was ambiguous. The PQ had been reelected overwhelmingly in April 1981, but only after pledging not to hold a second referendum on independence without new elections, thus making explicit the distinction between a mandate to govern and a mandate to move toward independence. Hard-liners within the party, angered by Quebec's defeat in the Constitutional negotiations, had renewed their pressure; in response to this increasingly independentist drift, Lévesque threatened to resign from the PQ unless his party backed him in his insistence on achieving independence only through majority rule. He called for a mail-in referendum, to be held on February 6 and 7, 1982. Ninety-five percent of the respondents supported Lévesque; however they represented less than half of the party's membership. In addition, Claude Morin, a PQ moderate, had left the cabinet, charging that the "collusion of Trudeau's government with English Canada" at the constitutional convention had so demoralized him that he could no longer continue to negotiate for Quebec.[62] With both the "étapiste" and "accommodationist" strategies defeated, Morin had little choice; however, he promised to continue to advise the Lévesque government from his old post at the University of Quebec. He was succeeded by Jacques-Yvan Morin.

The consequences for Quebec of these dramatic events were not yet known. With patriation, it is possible that the choices available to Quebec will become clearer and that the exercise of that choice—perhaps the most significant value in contemporary Quebec—will be more authentic even than that expressed in the referendum.

NOTES

1. André Bernard, *What Does Quebec Want?* (Toronto: James Lorimer and Company, 1978), p. 11.

2. November 23, 1886 as quoted in Wade, p. 419.

3. Bernard, *What Does Quebec Want?*, pp. 13–14.

4. *Courrier du Canada*, March 9, 1892, as quoted in Wade, p. 431.

5. Bernard, *What Does Quebec Want?*, pp. 1–16.

6. Rioux, *Quebec in Question*, p. 69.

7. Bernard, *What Does Quebec Want?*, p. 15.

8. Howard L. Singer, "The Institutionalization of Protest: The Quebec Separatist Movement" (Ph.D. diss., New York University, 1976), pp. 40–44.

9. André d'Allemagne *Le RIN et les débuts du mouvement indépendantist québécois* (Montreal: Editions de l'Etincelle, 1974), pp. 139–41.

10. Marcel Chaput, *Why I Am a Separatist*, transl. by Robert A. Taylor (Toronto: The Ryerson Press, 1961).

11. Singer, "Institutionalization of Protest,", p. 71.

12. Ibid., p. 112.

13. Nick Auf der Maur, " 'We're Winning': Bourgault; 'On est capable': Partisans," *Montreal Gazette*, August 4, 1967, as quoted in Singer, p. 138.

14. Singer, "Institutionalization of Protest," pp. 140–41.

15. René Lévesque, *An Option for Quebec* (Toronto: McClelland and Stewart, 1968), p. 11.

16. Ibid., p. 19.

17. Ibid., p. 27.

18. Ibid., p. 32.

19. Ibid., pp. 40–47.

20. Singer, "Institutionalization of Protest," p. 154.

21. Ibid., p. 161.

22. John T. Saywell, *The Rise of the Parti Québécois* (Toronto: University of Toronto Press, 1977), p. 32.

23. As quoted in Saywell, *Rise of the Parti Québécois*, p. 37.

24. Saywell, *Rise of the Parti Québécois*, pp. 44, 46–47.

25. Singer, "Institutionalization of Protest," pp. 203–4.

26. *Quand nous serons vraiment chez nous* (Montreal: Les Editions du Parti Québécois, 1973).

27. Ibid., p. 13.

28. Ibid., p. 14.

29. Maurice Pinard and Richard Hamilton, "The Independence Issue and the Polarization of the Quebec Electorate," *Canadian Journal of Political Science* 10 (1978):215–59, 228–29.

30. Pinard and Hamilton, "The Parti Québécois Comes to Power," *Canadian Journal of Political Science* 11 (1978):739–53, 744–45.

31. Saywell, *Rise of the Parti Québécois*, p. 97.

32. *Le Devoir*, October 8, 1975, as quoted in Singer, p. 257.

33. Parti Québécois, *The Parti Québécois Program (A Summary)*, Montreal: Les Editions du Parti Québécois, 1976.

34. As quoted in Saywell, *Rise of the Parti Québécois*, p. 141.

35. Pinard and Hamilton, "The Parti Québécois Comes to Power," p. 756.

36. Claude Morin, *Quebec Versus Ottawa: The Struggle for Self-Government 1960–72* (Toronto: University of Toronto Press, 1976), pp. 65–72.

37. Saywell, *Rise of the Parti Québécois*, p. 130.

38. Pinard and Hamilton, "The Parti Québécois Comes to Power," pp. 740–41; Saywell, p. 131.

39. Saywell, *Rise of the Parti Québécois*, p. 171.

40. David Butler and Donald Stokes, *Political Change in Britain* (New York: St. Martin's Press, 1971), pp. 175–78.

41. John Miesel, *Cleavages, Parties and Values in Canada*, Sage Professional Papers in Contemporary Sociology, vol. 1, no. 06-003 (London and Beverly Hills, Calif.: Sage Publications).

42. See also John H. Pammett, Lawrence LeDuc, Jane Jenson, and Harold D. Clarke, "The Perception and Impact of Issues in the 1974 Federal Election," *Canadian Journal of Political Science* 10 (1977):93–126.

43. Lawrence LeDuc, "The Issue of Majority Government in Two Federal Elections," *Canadian Journal of Political Science* 10 (1977):316.

44. Lawrence LeDuc and Walter H. White, "The Role of Opposition in a One-Party Dominant System: The Case of Ontario," *Canadian Journal of Political Science* 7 (1974):88–100.

45. Saywell, pp. 172–73.

46. Parti Québécois, *Official Program of the Parti Québécois*, 1978 ed., p. 7.

47. The following material is based on data published in the *New York Times*, the Toronto *Globe and Mail*, *La Presse*, *Maclean's*, and *Quebec Update*, a news release published weekly by the Quebec Government House, New York, 1978–present.

48. Parti Québécois, *D'Egal à Egal* (Among Equals) (Montreal, 1979).

49. Statement by the Prime Minister to the Assemblée Nationale, June 21, 1979, mimeographed, p. 3.

50. Quebec Government, Executive Council, *Quebec-Canada: A New Deal* (Quebec City: L'Editeur Official du Québec, 1979), p. 44.

51. Ibid.

52. Ibid., pp. 54–57.

53. Ibid., pp. 57–64.

54. Maurice Pinard and Richard Hamilton, "Quebec Public Opinion and Constitutional Reform," in Calvin Veltman, ed., *Contemporary Quebec* (Montreal: Les Presses de l'Université de Québec à Montréal, 1981), p. 120.

55. As reproduced in Elliot J. Feldman, ed., *The Quebec Referendum: What Happened and What Next? A Dialogue the Day After with Claude Forget and Daniel Latouche, May 21, 1980* (Cambridge, Mass.: University Consortium for Research on North America, Harvard University, 1980), p. 6.

56. Quebec, Liberal Party, Constitutional Committee, *A New Canadian Federation* (Montreal: Parti Libéral de Québec, 1980), p. 9.

57. Ibid., p. 10.

58. Ibid., pp. 21 ff.

59. Ibid., p. 135.

60. Jane Jacobs, *The Question of Separatism: Quebec and the Struggle over Sovereignty* (New York: Random House, 1980), p. 83.

61. See Claude Morin, "The Constitutional Orientation of the Government of Quebec," Speech in the National Assembly, May 28, 1981, in Veltman, *Contemporary Quebec*.

62. Claude Morin to Rene Lévesque, December 15, 1981.

Part 2
Eleven Ways of Looking at Separatism

4 • Personal Response

The following interviews vividly illustrate the attraction of the independence movement to eleven very different people. In each case, the very existence of the movement has had an impact on their lives. In some instances this impact has been profound; in others, it has been more superficial. Some of the people described here have been intensely committed to independence and have been closely involved in its organization; six of them were members of the Parti Québécois; the others were favorably inclined toward the movement and planned to vote for PQ candidates in the next election. Another, while rejecting the independence "option," felt that its existence was definitely beneficial.

The appeal of the independence movement varies according to the life experience of each individual. If there is one single fact that stands out upon reading the results of these interviews, it is the extent to which each person functions as an integrity within the overall political, social, and cultural context. The specific needs addressed by the movement, the intensity of the satisfaction gained, and the interrelations among these needs and benefits can be understood only in the context of each individual case history. This is particularly true for people whose satisfaction tends to be focused on a single value such as respect or enlightenment, as, for example, Sebastian Dupré or Paul Martin. In all cases, the appeal of the movement to a complex and highly individual pattern of social and emotional needs, and the gains that the individuals realized, was what clinched their commitment to it.

Nevertheless, certain trends may be discerned. As indicated in the first chapter, the historical context imposes certain conditions. The need to survive and the subtle, concurrent and sometimes opposing theme of autonomy, the dominance of the Church, and the isolation and later alienation of Quebecers from their English-speaking counterparts have all influenced the way in which gains or losses are experienced. Certain interrelations tend to recur; these may be called "facilitative relationships." For example, a number of

the people interviewed had experienced a lack of respect on the part
of English-speaking Canadians. In many cases this was translated
into low self-esteem. They credited the independence movement
with having improved their understanding of Quebec's social and
economic predicament to the extent that their self-esteem was
raised considerably. In such cases, the value, Enlightenment, may
be identified as facilitating Respect. Other facilitative relationships
may be observed between Respect and Power, Power and Enlightenment, Power and Well-being, and Enlightenment and Affection.
The dominance of these values may indicate a good deal about the
specific appeal of the movement.

The case studies describe the response of twelve individuals to
the independence movement. Each person was asked about its positive or negative effects on his or her life in terms of each of the six
values defined in chapter 1. In addition, each was questioned about
the impact of the movment on the "average French Canadian." At
the end of the interview the respondent was asked about his own
attitudes and about the degree of his involvement in the movement.
The interviews varied in length but averaged between one and one
and one-half hours. They were recorded on tape wherever possible.
The respondents were encouraged to express their opinions as
freely as they wished and even to digress. The result was a rich and
suggestive series of case studies that are presented in the pages that
follow.

INTERVIEW 7: SEBASTIAN DUPRÉ, PARISH PRIEST

"Saint John the Baptist: a small blond boy with a sheep! To me
that is an example of submission. The real Saint John the Baptist is
not a small boy but an immense colossus who sees the whole world.
He knows where he is going." Sebastian Dupré shares the same
lonely perspective as this patron of French Canada. He has re-
nounced earthly pursuits to free others, in turn, from "depen-
dency" and to bring to his universe the message of liberation. He is
frail, dedicated, intense, compelling. The same uneasiness that led
him to the seminary now directs his intensity to the issue of
Separatism.

"When I entered the seminary, what I cared about, what interested me above all, was that people should be happy, that they find
joy within themselves. That was a long time ago." His realization

that he could not live on divine grace alone came in the period after ordination, when he was assigned to a parish in downtown Montreal. It was a poor parish: of three thousand families, seven hundred were on welfare. Nevertheless, he said, it was a coveted assignment. Sebastian said Mass, heard confessions, and performed other prescribed duties. "But the day I realized that we cannot talk about love if we cannot talk about justice, if we cannot talk about sharing with the poor slobs here below . . . I began to have trouble." Sebastian began to speak out against the injustices he perceived, and was transferred to his present Siberia, an impoverished parish in a dreary industrial area on the fringe of Montreal, but, most important, in a district which had already elected a Péquiste to the National Assembly. Here his views, if they continued to contaminate souls, at least could steal no new seat for the Parti Québécois.

In the six years since his ordination Sebastian has come to realize that "the government in power, the police, the Church hierarchy, the banks are all in the same bag [*dans un seul sac*]," yet he feels no bitterness toward them. "I personally have the impression . . . that they are blind in their sincerity; they do not see that certain actions mean a continuance of enslavement." Separatism can change this, be believes. In economic and social terms, it plays a critical role, "because there is a passage in the gospels, in the Bible which says, 'The spirit of the Lord saw me bring good news to the poor. It saw me soothe the hearts of the wounded, break the chains of those who are enslaved, open the eyes of those who are blind.'" Separatism is thus a means of carrying out the will of God, for it brings the same benefits, and has the same functions as, the good works prescribed by scripture, in terms of wealth, well-being, power, and information.

As a priest, he is still in a position to enlighten others, for since his exile to the Parish of St. Hubert, the hierarchy has left him alone. "Now, I say what I think, in church or in the street." He tries to get others to express their needs, by working with community groups and he has also organized a clothing cooperative and worked with legal-aid lawyers. "Today I realize that in order to find joy . . . one must begin by rejecting everything that enslaves, that makes one dependent [*irresponsable*]. . . . It is not enough to be happy, to find joy. I mean that from now on one must be free. When I see someone who is enslaved—who is dependent on Bingo [a reference to fund-raising in his former parish, which he opposed], on Quebec, on the Church, on having a wife, who is not free, it saddens me. For this reason, when I see a world which depends on a political regime, it makes me very sad. There is only one place where there is no enslavement, and that is within the Parti Québécois. Perhaps one day there will be, but not now." Unlike the Church, which had disappointed him, the Parti Québécois offered him the freedom to liberate others.

But for him, Separatism is more than the Parti. "It's that, but it's more than that. It's everything which gives people—which permits them to begin thinking . . . on their life, their future. . . . Separatism is giving people an urge to invent a future, to invent tomorrow, then the day after, then to find solutions. . . . God tells us, I have made you in my image, then in my likeness. God—this is someone who is a Creator, this is someone who is inventive, this is someone who is not set in his ways, but who finds a thousand new ways to do what he wants!" Separatism, it seems, is a way of being all that he can be—of imitating God.

Sebastian felt that he had relinquished any current claim to power, as a result of supporting the movement, because "there are many, many people who are not Separatist." He seemed to discount his influence in the community, both because it was the result of a new loss on his part, and because, I think, he could not equate the power of prophesy with the power of influence. He could not consider his moral and intellectual leadership as power any more than he could view the spiritual leadership of St. John the Baptist as power. Unconsciously, he saw himself as a prophet.

Nevertheless, Sebastian Dupré clearly has a role to play in Church politics. Three months after his transfer to St. Hubert he was elected to the collegial body which represents the 800 priests in the Diocese of Montreal. Of twenty-two representatives Sebastian was elected by the highest majority, which, he said, indicates that there are many others who think as he does. Because of the way in which the seats are apportioned (the priests are divided first according to occupation and then according to age; and each casts a single vote, in his own division), Sebastian's victory would seem also to indicate that his politics have brought him a higher degree of influence among his peers, in this instance, parish pastors in the thirty-to-forty age group. Sebastian was, in fact, referred to by a Church official as "the leader of the young, eager priests."

Sebastian's conflict with the Church hierarchy has, in fact, extended his influence beyond the Church. He writes frequently for newspapers and other periodicals. On the day I interviewed him, a guest editorial of his appeared in *Le Devoir*.

Although Sebastian claims to have no power, he actually has the type of power he values most, even though it is not the type of power the establishment values most. His influence is significant also because it brings power not only to himself but also to the Separatist movement and is therefore one of the ways in which Separatism sustains itself.

As far as information was concerned, being Separatist required one to scrutinize an unpleasant situation. It "obliges us to be much, much more attentive to what is going on," in order not to make the same mistakes again and in order to consider what might replace the present structure. As he said earlier, Separatism "lets us invent tomorrow."

Sebastian was hesitant to talk about respect for himself; he seemed, in fact, to feel that he had lost much respect from others as the result of his political involvement. Yet, if he had incurred a net loss of approval, both by Church officials who had attempted to silence him and by others who disagreed with his political opinions and behavior, it would be difficult to say that he had suffered a net loss of respect. His transfer to St. Hubert indicated that to some degree the Church hierarchy had taken him seriously; when I asked a Church official for the name of a Separatist priest, he immediately—and with no discernible sign of disrespect—referred me to Sebastian. The number of individuals who respected Sebastian may have diminished; even so, it seems likely that the feelings of those who do respect him are deeper and more genuine, based not on his status as a priest or pastor, but on actions and commitments with which they can either sympathize and identify or take issue, as the case may be. He seemed to derive a great deal of self-respect, not so much from the movement itself as through his own involvement in it. It had helped him to achieve an identity of his own, through conflict with his superiors. It had given him a role which not only enabled him to incorporate his religious vocation with his social perceptions, but brought him satisfaction as well.

Separatism had also brought him affection, which was important because of the feeling of "togetherness" it gave him. "One is no longer alone, one feels stronger. . . . I do not like to be alone, alone in my opinion, alone on my road. . . . I find it important to feel I'm with others. It's just because of that I can feel that if I make a mistake [there are others who can help me]." He had found the affection he needed in the Parti Québécois and in the Separatist movement, especially among young people in the eighteen-to-twenty-one age group.

It was my impression that, had there been no Separatist issue, Sebastian would have clung to some lonely perspective, both because he is an unusually perceptive and sensitive person and because within the milieu of the Church it is one means of retaining one's individual identity. The Separatist movement gave him support through the companionship and affection of others, and was therefore extremely important to his emotional well-being.

INTERVIEW 12: JACQUES ROCHE, TEACHER

Jacques Roche earned his Ph.D. in Sociology several years ago. He teaches each summer at the University of Montreal; from September through June, however, he is employed at the CEGEP, a publicly supported institution encompassing the "twelfth" and "thirteenth" grades. These were established by the province in 1964, as part of the Liberal party's sweeping educational reform. There is now one in nearly every major town. Together with the elementary and secondary school systems, they are under the jurisdiction of the Minister of Education and are represented by the same union.

Although his answers reflect the intellectual predispositions of a sociologist, Jacques feels that his reactions have much in common with those of teachers at all levels of the school system. He speaks frequently of the "educational milieu." To the extent then that an individual can be considered representative of his milieu, Jacques Roche speaks for other teachers as well.

The single most important and most positive effect of the Separatist movement has been its integrating tendency, Jacques believes. He points to a new social cohesiveness, experienced chiefly in terms of a new "collective dimension" in interpersonal relationships. This factor has increased his own economic and political power, but its most important effect has been to improve the self-respect and national pride of all French Canadians, and it "has added something to the affection and other sentiments one feels, whether toward individuals or groups."

Separatism—or independentism, as many *Péquistes* prefer to call it—has provided an element of cohesion in the educational milieu, "certainly, if you take the labor movement, at the moment when we needed cohesion to make our salary demands. In particular, in 1972, when we went on strike with all government employees—210,000 at the same time, of which 70,000 were teachers . . . I think that the fact of feeling as Quebecers had a certain influence on [our] actions which enabled us to seek more than the government offered us." There have also been other, indirect economic benefits, including the summer and other part-time teaching jobs at the university. He was able to get these partly because the curriculum chairman knew of his political affiliation through a student they had both had. As Jacques explains it, "Things equal to the same thing are equal to each other; opportunities for employment are better when an employer has the same tendencies."

He does not feel that the economy of Quebec has made any important advances as a result of Separatism. The campaign to "buy French Canadian," to spend one's money in Quebec has not been very successful, chiefly because of the disparity between the needs of the consumer and Quebec's ability to produce. However, he credits a decision by Hydro-Québec, a public power corporation, to spend its money within the province whenever possible to this trend and to the general tendency toward social and economic cohesiveness.

Personal power is not especially important for Jacques. He thinks Separatism is capable of giving him more power, since the general opinion in his milieu is pro-Separatist, pro-Parti Québécois, and the majority of his students worked for the Parti Québécois in the 1970 provincial election. In situations outside the classroom, "personal opinions are an element of popularity and therefore of power." But he sees himself more as a counsellor, or mentor, and committee assignments and executive positions do not interest him. As a social scientist, his code of ethics prevents him from using the profession as a vehicle for his personal opinions. Consciously he makes no attempt to use his position as a *Péquiste* to gain power, although his influence and popularity with the students are clearly a source of satisfaction to him. Like Sebastian Dupré, he claims not to be interested in personal power, and he believes that political power can exist only on a "collective" level.

Much more important for Jacques have been the self-respect and national pride that he feels as a result of the Separatist movement. Implicit in respect for other French Canadians is respect for oneself. Jacques feels that Separatism "has given something to the individual and to the collectivity," and that "this collective dimension is fundamental. Formerly, we saw ourselves only as individuals, and each one tried to earn his daily bread, each one tried to produce, in an individualist, capitalist silence." The facility to think in collective terms, which is the greatest contribution of

Separatism, also distinguishes Separatists from the vast majority of anti-Separatists and non-Separatists.

Jacques thought there was little chance that he and other Separatists would ever accept any of the solutions proposed by Prime Minister Trudeau or Premier Bourassa. These men, he believed, failed to deal with the real issue because they neglect the "collective dimension" and view the problems of French Canadians essentially as individual ones. As an example, Jacques points out, Trudeau hoped to save Canadian federalism by means that would enable each individual to deal in his own way with problems of language and culture. Language courses were offered in a program heavily subsidized by the federal and provincial governments, but this, in his opinion, "fell totally to the side of the question because it offered an individual solution to a problem which is collective."

The problem is collective, he believes, because "it is perceived in a collective fashion. A situation can be defined objectively, of course, but it is defined subjectively, also, by the perspective people give it." If Quebecers, or any other group, perceive themselves in this way, they are what they wish to be, collectively, and to consider them as individuals does not deal adequately with their needs. Jacques thinks that the movement has defined, and thus helped to create this collectivity.

He finds also that his own subjective reality is most in conformity with the reality defined by others who believe in Separatism, and in particular by the Parti Québécois. This corroborates one of the main hypotheses of this study, which is that the success of the movement and of the PQ is directly proportionate to the degree and extent to which its "objective" reality conforms with the "subjective" reality of the people of Quebec. For Jacques, it would seem that the movement offers something more: in making it possible for French Canadians to see themselves as a "collectivity," it implies that they are worthy of recognition and respect as such, and not only as individuals.

The "collective consciousness" seems to have had a profound and positive effect also on Jacques's intellectual orientation. For one thing, it offered a new and more concrete alternative to the ideology of pluralism—an ideology that was becoming more and more difficult to accept as his interest in French Canadian history focused increasingly on the period from 1830 to 1840. Separatism, he believes, has been responsible for this shift in interest from the mythical "golden age" before the Conquest to the nationalism and struggles for independence of the 1830s. It is clear that the painful experience of 1837—and the lesson that coexistence, if not supported by an ideology of pluralism, would be imposed by brute force—was easier for him to accept, both because of the emotional support that this collective consciousness gave him, and the option that it provided. In addition, it was clear from the context of the interview that this collective consciousness made it possible for him to accept his historical past and the specific conditions that differentiated French Canadians from their English-speaking counterparts. It convinced him that his own political and social perceptions were not only a product of his professional orientation as a sociologist, but had an objective reality as well, (for to him, "objectivity is simply many objectivities"), and this gave him a great deal of intellectual satisfaction.

Separatism had helped people to feel closer to one another, he thought, and had made for more relaxed relationships with others—particularly other Separatists. There was a new understanding of one another: "We can communicate now by understatement, by irony, and that adds something." But, he added, "Naturally I don't choose my friends for their politics. I have as good friends among the Liberals as I do among the Separatists."

Jacques's perception of Separatism as an integrating factor in Quebec may be attributed to his training as a sociologist, but his experience of it in terms of a "collective consciousness" tells more about the way Separatism satisfies his own needs. His professional background together with his formal interest in the interview situation dictated highly intellectualized responses to the questions asked, and his professional self-esteem may well require a theoretical explanation for the emotional satisfaction that he derives from being a Separatist. The "collective consciousness" concept is sufficiently general to describe Separatism's overall function for him, and it also indicates how Separatism contributes to his sense of Well-being. Intellectually, it does him credit. But there is something more. The "collective consciousness" that he describes is more than a pleasant intellectual experience, more than a general factor. It describes a deeply felt affective relationship with other French Canadians, one that because of its intensity, is perhaps more easily expressed in general terms. Through the "collective consciousness" that it promotes, then, Separatism does more than define a new collectivity; it helps to define a new object of affection, based more on individual relationships than on territorial or even historical considerations. This feeling of belonging, this intense emotional response was what made each of the other functions

meaningful and gave him a sense of inner tranquility unlike anything he had experienced before.

INTERVIEW 15: ROGER, SALESMAN

I first saw Roger in the doorway of his friend's rented vacation
cottage. He wore a navy-blue tee shirt with yellow sleeves, and his
hair was dirty. He was listening to a portable radio while two
young women sat on folding chairs, playing chess. I sensed that he
had nothing urgent to do, and walked over and asked if anyone
there was a Separatist. All three looked confused, one or two
smiled, and all three said no. I said that I was also interested in the
opinions of federalists. The two women turned back to their chess
game. Roger said he was not a federalist, and that he was driving
back to Montreal that evening and would have to leave within an
hour.

I got him to talk by telling him about my difficulty in meeting
people who were willing to express their opinions for a book I was
writing. How, in his opinion, could I get the information I needed?
He asked to see my questionnaire. Although the questions were
written in English, he had no difficulty with them, but he spoke
only French to me. His accent was provincial and hard to understand, but he answered every question, some in detail. As we
spoke, it began to rain and the others went inside. We stood on the
doorstep, barely sheltered. Since he had not actually accepted the
interview I did not ask to turn on my tape recorder, fearing that this
would cause him to terminate the interview. When he had finished,
I told him that there were certain answers I had not fully understood, and asked if he would come over to my cottage to record
them over a beer. He said he would be over in five minutes, but
never came. Later I saw him playing ball in the road. The responses, which I recorded from memory within an hour of the
interview, are therefore brief, and there may be certain minor inac-
curacies due to difficulties with the language and the fact that they
were not recorded simultaneously. Nevertheless, the intereview
has value in that it is entirely spontaneous. The responses are even
more spontaneous than the subject realized since he did not come to
terms with the fact that he was being interviewed. When he declined to answer my questionnaire, I presented him with the option
of answering it as an informant. He was thus able to give the
answers he wanted me to hear without expressly committing him-

self as their source. I believe he was unaware of the degree to which he was expressing his own opinions, and that because of this the answers are unusually candid.

Roger S. is twenty-five years old and a salesman for Xerox. He has never been active in politics. Although he votes in provincial and federal elections, and voted for the PQ in 1970 and planned to again in 1973, he did not consider himself a Separatist. Dedicated revolutionaries are Separatists, he believes, but he is not. Separatist attitudes are "extremist." On the other hand, a federalist is someone who votes federalist, and his attitudes are chiefly wanting other federalists to control Quebec. That leaves Roger (and a considerable portion of the population of Quebec) with no political identification. Roger did not tell me how his friend or his girlfriend had voted, but he did say that he would be on better terms with them if he supported Separatism. Young people voted for the Parti Québécois. Roger did so because if he supported the opposite party he would lose the affection *(sympathie)* of his friends. He thought that French Canadians were better respected now, chiefly by those in Ottawa and the English (-speaking Canadians). He was not sure if any French Canadians were less respected now, possibly extremists such as the Rose brothers because they murdered Laporte. Perhaps all French Canadians respected them less; they gave Separatism a bad name. He felt the average French Canadian had more self-respect, but he could not explain why. Would he gain more respect, in current terms, from supporting Separatism or federalism? That depended. The question was unclear. It depended whether I meant personally or collectively, and also from whom. Collectively he certainly got more respect, but individually it depended on whether he was dealing with a Separatist or a federalist. The average French Canadian definitely had more self-respect, but Roger could not explain why.

Roger told me that because there were now two parties in competition with one another, they had to compete for votes. For this reason, he said, one could answer yes to my question: the average French Canadian is better informed, and, he supposed, he might be too; that seemed to follow. But he could not say that he would be better informed as a result of supporting either Separatism or federalism; that question was meaningless. One did not learn anything by voting; one voted on the basis of information already obtained.

Separatism gave him someone to vote for. Although it offered no immediate economic benefits, and might even bring hardship in the short run, ultimately Quebec would develop a strong economy of her own and everything would be all right. In terms of political power, the advantages were more immediate: he could express his dissatisfaction with the Liberal party, which was run by people fifty and sixty years old. He was not a member of the PQ, but he was in sufficient agreement with the party to vote for it, and he thought that by doing so he was adding more power to it, with the result of a net gain in personal power. Would this power diminish if there were no such thing as Separatism? "Yes."

Roger was confident that the PQ would win within five years, and that Quebec would become independent, probably economically as well as politically, as the result of a parliamentary victory. His overt attitude, if pro-independence, was less than enthusiastic. It seemed to me that he had voted *Péquiste* mainly to express his dissatisfaction with the Liberal party, and with the "establishment" in general, and that insofar as independence was concerned, it was best to wait and see.

Roger's face was indistinguishable from many I saw in Quebec—not in terms of its physiognomy so much as expression, the vacant eyes, the flaccid, usually open mouth. Had I not asked his age, I would have taken him for a high-school student. There was a surprisingly young quality about him, not only in appearance but in the way he behaved and spoke. There was no intensity, no urgency to express himself on any of the subjects we touched. I hesitate to say that he was alienated and disaffected; there was not sufficient evidence in an interview under such circumstances. But there was a very evident lack of commitment. This was shown by his unwillingness to identify himself with either faction, although he did vote PQ and planned to again. It is possible, of course, that there were many in Quebec who were willing to vote *Péquiste*, but unwilling to join the party, feeling that membership in the PQ presented greater personal risk than membership in the Liberal party or the Union Nationale. It is also unlikely that, even if he did consider himself a Separatist, he would have identified himself as such to an Anglophone.

One wonders to what degree this reluctance to identify himself reflects a deeper lack of commitment and ultimately to what degree this attitude represented that of a good many other Québécois. In defining "Separatist" and "federalist," he implied that a large number of French Canadians have no more political commitment than he. Whether these people did, like Roger, vote PQ in subsequent elections depends on how successfully the party recruited their votes.

Roger seemed to like the present competition between parties, because it brought him both power and information. In answering my questions, he said spontaneously several times that the existence of the two factions was beneficial. He enjoyed the competition for his vote, and he liked being in a position to add power to the Parti Québécois. This may explain his lack of commitment. Nevertheless, it was clear that his sympathies were with the PQ. He was dissatisfied with the Liberal party, he said, and the PQ had given him a choice. Presented with that choice, he rejected the Liberals and voted with the *Péquistes*. It is uncertain whether he would have voted at all had there been no choice. For this reason, it appeared likely that Roger would continue to vote PQ as long as it remained an opposition party. Whether he has continued to support the party now that it is in power or voted *oui* in the 1980 referendum is uncertain.

INTERVIEW 18: PHILIPPE BEAUSÉJOUR, PROVINCIAL BUREAUCRAT

Philippe Beauséjour is a provincial bureaucrat, the tenth child of a federal judge. An aloof but amiable manner, a seriousness that belies his thirty-three years, and an impeccable *toilette* give the impression of an eighteenth-century gentleman and serve to remind anyone who might be interested that here is a member of one of the most influential families in Quebec. The ambience of his comfortable townhouse in Montreal, where the interview took place, is a pleasant blend of *habitant* and what might be recognized in New York as Upper West Side.

With a Liberal government in power, it seemed somewhat ironic that Philippe held a responsible position in the ministry of intergovernmental affairs. His former deputy minister, Claude Morin, had quit his post in 1971 when he switched from the Liberal party to the PQ, but at Philippe's level it was still possible to be a *Péquiste*.

There are no available statistics as to the number of Separatists in the provincial bureaucracy, but I was told that the ranks were "honeycombed with them." In private conversation, Philippe is frank about his politics. Nevertheless, he is careful to protect himself against any possible conflict of interest. His caution is interest-

ing because it is one example of the context in which much of the
PQ's political activity took place in the years before it assumed
power. As a civil servant, Philippe was enjoined from participating
in any kind of political activity. But as a *Péquiste*, he faced a more
difficult problem, that of commitment to a political movement
dedicated to removing not only the particular government he
worked for, but its constitutional basis as well. The nature of the
conflict, which he faced daily, was not merely political; it was
constitutional. There were, in addition, some menacing overtones.
The October Crisis, adverse publicity by the Liberal party, fear of
economic chaos, and ignorance of the PQ's platform combined,
with the result that the Parti Québécois was regarded as unsound
and even subversive by many French Canadians. Many Péquistes
were therefore reluctant to identify themselves as such. This
heightened the political and constitutional conflict in which
Philippe found himself.

He appeared to have resolved the problem successfully, through
dealing with the conflict in two main ways. The first was conventional: he drew a careful distinction between "personal" and "political" relationships, applying it even to relative minutiae. The
interview is an example. He agreed to meet me because I was a
friend of his sister, who worked as a librarian in New York, but he
would not see me at his office during working hours. He insisted on
setting up the interview as if it were a social event: I was to come
with my husband, and children if necessary, but not alone. During
our conversation he offered to arrange interviews with various persons, including Claude Morin, whom he knew personally, but he
stopped short at René Lévesque, whom he did not know (although
it would have been feasible for him to do so).

The second is more original: Philippe reconciled the conflict, on
the one hand, with the advantages, on the other, of being a *Péquiste*
working for a Liberal government. Because of his political commitment, he believed, he was a better civil servant, even under the
present government, although he regarded this as a transient phase
in the history of Quebec. His involvement in the movement, he
said, provided a great stimulus to his work for the government of
Quebec. It helped him in planning the work of his department, in
understanding federal-provincial relations, and, most of all, "it is
important in defining a new Quebec. . . . If I work for a government that is susceptible to change, I believe that the role of bureaucrat is to assure the continuity of the state, not at all to engage in

active politics, whether it's the Parti Québécois, the Liberal party or the Union Nationale. If I wanted to engage in active politics, I would relinquish my commitment, I would find another profession."

Philippe felt that he had less power, personally, because of his membership in the party. "I am not in the circles of power. I would gain much more power from supporting federalism, first, because this ideology is forbidden by the party which is presently my employer, and I would gain much more . . . working for another government." Nevertheless, he thought that Quebec, particularly the provincial Liberal party, had gained leverage, as a result, in its dealings with Ottawa: "The development of the idea of independence in Quebec, the strength of Separatism, is an extremely important factor in the power of Quebec and its government to negotiate with the rest of Canada—both the federal government and other, provincial governments—in the sense that it provides an alternative to the present Provincial government. More precisely, the Parti Québécois can direct the government. I mean the federal structure, in its discussions with the present [provincial] government, must always come back to the realization of this factor, and not put the government of Quebec in a bad position. So we see that on such points as social welfare and health the federal government has had to make concessions, in order to agree on policies that will be acceptable to the present government of Quebec. Well, that is an enormous strength . . . for the government of Quebec to be able to say to the Federal government, 'Fine, if you don't treat us nicely, that's just too bad [and] M. Lévesque . . . will be the next premier.' That gives an enormous amount of power . . . to the government for which I work."

Beauséjour also believed that the movement had brought power to certain organizations, including trade unions and other "grassroots" organizations. Its existence coincided with an awakening, a consciousness—social, economic, and political—with the result that its ideas were discussed in new milieux. Not only had these ideas become influential in new sectors of Quebec society, but Beauséjour thought that they had brought enormous power to "pressure groups."

Intellectually, the movement had brought Beauséjour enormous satisfaction and self-respect. During the interview, his repeated, spontaneous, and enthusiastic discussion of French Canadian culture indicated that his awareness of it was more than sufficient to offset the present political and economic disadvantages of being a *Péquiste*. In contrast with many of the cases studied, the movement did not serve as a substitute for formal education; Beauséjour is one of the elite, having studied both history and law at Laval University. Nevertheless, the movement clearly had a social function very similar to that served by formal education among many elite groups elsewhere (but neglected by the educational hierarchy in Quebec): awareness of self in relation to environment, not ony in a physical sense but in cultural terms as well.

In this respect, there was a subtle but profound similarity in the function of Separatism for both the elite and the masses. In both cases, the movement brought knowledge. In Beauséjour's case, the chief benefit of this enlightenment was self-respect; in most others, it was knowledge and, indirectly, self-respect. "The movement has brought much more 'self-respect' and that has brought much more respect . . . to the masses of French Canadians. This is extremely positive, because the French Canadians can be proud. They have their writers, their cineasts, their songwriters, their businessmen, and their own things are going well."

For Beauséjour, self-respect was more important than, and often a prerequisite for, the respect of others. "There is a Quebec civilization, but I don't think there is a Canadian civilization. Canadian culture is defined primarily in reference to American culture, not by itself. Quebec culture exists in and of itself. That is a rather fundamental difference. I think that Quebecers, French Canadians, are more respected, but in consequence they are perhaps more detested, perhaps more difficult, more annoying, to the other Canadians, but they are more respected; I think it is important to respect oneself. I think it is more important."

Beauséjour was eighteen when Charles de Gaulle came to power in France, and he traces the origin of the present Separatist movement to that period. There were two main consequences of de Gaulle's rise to power. First, the attainment of independence by other French-speaking nations, such as Algeria and the Congo, made it possible for French Canadians as well to consider independence as a real possibility. A second, more salient one was that, with France's political resurgence, Beauséjour and others felt that they were no longer pawns in Great Britain's politics with the United States, no longer battered survivors of a defunct political culture. "We ceased being ashamed to say that we belonged to a French culture. . . . [Not having] governments which changed every six months put France in a new perspective, with the result that we were less troubled, we were no longer ashamed to say that we spoke the same language, shared the same intellectual spirit as the French."

If Beauséjour's intellectual involvement paralleled his political involvement in the cause of independence, it is nevertheless clear that his intellectual satisfaction was augmented not only by the limited political role he permitted himself, but by the success of the movement in general. It would thus be difficult to say that intellectual satisfaction was a direct result of his involvement. What was clear was that Beauséjour derived enormous self-respect through comprehension of the evolving political situation and that this congruence of consciousness and political action combined to give him a sense of well-being.

Beauséjour thought that the movement had generated more affection among Quebecers, and he did not qualify it by limiting it to *Péquistes*. By giving all individuals a deeper basis for self-respect, it had changed their relations with one another "distinctly." Not only is there the pleasure in discovering a new Quebec, but in discovering each other. It is extremely important to understand oneself, as it is to understand one's nation.

For Beauséjour, the movement is a means of resolving old conflicts, of coming to terms with an identity of which he can feel proud, and of sharing this unfolding awareness with people of similar intellectual concerns.

INTERVIEW 19: JEAN DUPONT, MECHANIC———

Jean Dupont operates a gas station on a highway in northern Quebec. I stopped there one afternoon to ask if there were any workers, either there or in the area, who were Separatist. Jean and his wife were working on a car. He doubted very much, he said, that there were any separatists in that region; Separatism was often accompanied by violence, and violence was a thing of the past. People did not want either now. I assured him that I did not think Separatism was violent, that, on the contrary, it was constructive, and that I had recently had lengthy conversations with some prominent members of the Parti Québécois. "I could tell you about the Parti Québécois," he said. I explained that I was aware of the party's history and platforms, and that his own reactions were of more interest to me. Would he be willing to talk with me sometime? We agreed to meet at the gas station the following night,

since he would be open until one, and there would be fewer inter-
ruptions. He was anxious that the proprietor not know of the interview, since he was "not sympathetic to the Parti Québécois," and
Jean was afraid of his reaction. The interview took place late in the
evening, while Jean's wife patiently took care of the customers. In
the back of the room a young couple drank beer and necked.
Neither Jean nor his wife took any notice of them, though they
remained there throughout the interview. Why they were there is
unclear. It is possible that Jean had some misgivings about the
nature and purpose of the interview, and felt he needed a witness,
but perhaps the cold weather had merely forced them in from their
car. The interview, which was done in English, took approximately
one hour and is punctuated with sounds from this couple and an
automatic gong.

Jean has been a member of the PQ for less than a year, having
been recruited by an acquaintance who is a sociology instructor and
a party activist. At twenty-eight, he is gaunt, almost Lincolnesque.
While he believes that independence is necessary for economic reasons, it became clear in the course of the conversation that membership in the party had already brought him a kind of "education" in
economics, and, as a result, considerable self-esteem. His education
within the party has given clarity and structure to an otherwise
hazy social situation in the economic terms that are meaningful to
him. It has also enabled him to speak convincingly and with a sense
of authority on a subject of great importance for him. It seemed
that this opportunity to talk about the economic situation in
Quebec also helps to alleviate his anxieties and does as much to
enhance his sense of well-being as the hope of an easier future.
Finally, the learning experienced through party membership in some
small way makes up for the formal education he missed. Although
he left school after the seventh grade, and repeatedly admits that he
is "not educated," he is obviously proud of his new knowledge, and
of the fact that he possesses an awareness that today's youth,
though more educated formally, do not have.

Jean's reasons for joining the party were based on his own economic needs. He believes that independence "absolutely must happen . . . because we can't exist. If you take the taxes we pay to the
federal and to the provincial government and you put both together, you have a certain amount, amount X, and then with the
expenditures of administering Quebec and sustaining the population of Quebec, with those two amounts you will have some 400
million dollars." He estimates that about 45 percent of the $100 he

earns weekly goes for taxes. "Do you know why? O.K. Let's say you earn $100. . . . Now then you take federal tax, provincial taxes. After that let's say you got left about $75 from a hundred. Now, you go downtown, you buy a pair of jeans. You pay eight percent. Now on that pair of jeans, there's another 12 percent that you don't see, but it's there anyway, if it's imported. And let's say for plywood and stuff like that you got another 12 percent, less 8 percent. That's 20 percent. So if you carry on like that you got left of your hundred dollars you earn every week—you got left about forty, fifty that you can spend." On gasoline the federal tax is thirty percent. "So if you take all that money that you pay to the federal government, and keep it in Quebec, you got it made. Half of the money we pay to the federal, they give it to the other provinces." He complained that the iron deposits of Seven Islands, Chibogamou, and Abitibi were shipped out of the provinces, chiefly to Europe. "We don't see it. . . . They make the metal and after that they sell it to us!" If independence comes, "if we got some intelligent people over there they'll keep the iron stuff and put it so you [Americans and Europeans] can't make things out of it. It costs less for building, it costs less for all stuff like that, and the province of Quebec owes money to, I don't know, to everybody, I guess. So, if we take all that stuff and put it together we'll pay all our debt. . . . Like other people who have refineries, why can't *we* have one over here?" He was not aware that the Aigle d'Or refinery was owned by French Canadians; he recognized it by its English name, Golden Eagle.

Jean feels he is better informed as the result of his contact with the party "because I believe in what they say and it makes sense." He repeated the argument against federal taxes. "I did learn a lot of things I didn't know." This is important to him. "I like to know where I'm going. If I don't know, I'll take my things and go back to the States."

He feels that he has more political power now, but that is less important to him. "I have a kind of power, but if there's like three million like me, that'll be power!" He believed that real power would come only when the PQ won control of the legislature.

Respect from others is not especially important for Jean. Like several of the respondents, he felt that one was respected or not respected according to whether his beliefs conformed with another's. His is obviously proud to be a *Péquiste*, but he keeps his politics to himself. "If I told everyone I was in the party I would lose half of my business." Nevertheless, he is sure enough of his own beliefs to accept fully the fact that others do not share them: "I guess they hate the Parti Québécois—it's kind of hard to make them change their minds."

Not only has Jean experienced more affection and loyalty from others, but he is able to feel more affection both toward Quebec and other French Canadians. "Four or five years ago before they started talking about Quebec and the PQ I didn't want to know anything about Quebec or Canada itself. It wasn't like I didn't believe in it . . . let's say I wasn't home for very long. Now I feel I'm getting home—more." He felt that the loyalty he gained from others believing in independence was very important to him, because "it feels more like home."

The notion of being "home" is important, both because of the significance it holds of Jean and because for its recurrence in Separatist literature.[1] For Jean Dupont, it appeared to have mitigated the sense of alienation—a condition that is a recurrent theme in these interviews. It would be impossible to comment extensively on alienation in Jean; the interview was not designed to study it and there was not sufficient spontaneous material. My impression, however, is that for a considerable period of his life Jean was unsure of his own identity—that is, he had neither a national identity nor a work identity.

Years of wandering, both in the United States and the Bahamas, made him fluent in English and helped him to forget, at least for the time being, the pain of being French Canadian. "When I was in the States, in the beginning I had an accent, but in the last two years I lost my accent. . . . People would ask, where are you from? and I would say, Oh, I'm from Canada. So I didn't want to say I was French Canadian. I wasn't anything at all." During that period he tried a number of different trades. "I have [taken] about thirty-six courses. You name it. I was even a barber." He did not say what prompted his return to Quebec, or when he returned. Nevertheless, it is clear that his involvement in the Separatist movement, culminating in joining the party, has given him the sense of national and, through it, personal identity that was lacking. He is an intelligent man, and the information he has gained as a result of the movement has enabled him to talk knowledgeably and intelligently with others, thus further enhancing a sense of belonging.

Jean believes in independence "*au bout* [all the way]," but his idea of independence is also reflective of the "*maîtres chez nous*" philosophy. "Independence means . . . like the English. We don't want to throw them out and stuff, we just want to be in Quebec, like

'Home Sweet Home.' We don't want to pay for the rest of the country.

It was my impression that Separatism had been of unusual help to Jean and that it so successfully filled his needs that he was able to relate to his milieu with an intensity and satisfaction that he would not otherwise have experienced.

INTERVIEW 22: EDGAR DION, OCTOGENARIAN————————————————————

Tall, reserved, and still severely handsome despite his eighty-three years, Edgar Dion received me at his home in Ste.-Foy, a suburb of Quebec. The brick bungalow was solidly built and immaculately tended, with the help of an unmarried daughter, I learned later. Inside, the furnishings were unpretentious almost to the point of austerity. The living and dining room reflected an asceticism depicted in paintings of nineteenth-century provincial life. I had the impression that furnishings had been bought only as needed. There were few upholstered pieces; most of them were simple oak. A large upright piano faced the entrance; on it were some books on the technique of playing the recorder. As for the smaller items—the little clues to the affective life of the person— they were curiously divided between the religious and the intellectual. On the piano was a statue of Minerva, but over the doorway to the dining room hung a plain wooden crucifix, the kind that hangs above the blackboard in every parochial schoolroom.

Dion answered my questions with the same detachment I had observed in other French Canadian intellectuals. His voice was steady, and his accent the closest to a Parisian French I had heard in Quebec. After considering each question, he replied with precise, and at times almost elegant, sentences. There was no intensity, no direct emotion expressed in the answers, but when confronted with certain questions, a mild case of Parkinson's disease caused his right hand to tremble.

Although a chemist by profession, all but five of Dion's professional years were spent in an academic setting. His long and distinguished career was, for the most part, removed from the tensions of the private sector of the economy, and there had been no prolonged competition, on a personal level, with English-speaking counterparts. There was no evidence of a negative identity created through painful competition with, and self-reflected appraisal by, an alien majority.

Dion was one of the few nonpolitical persons I interviewed who was confident of the strength of the Parti Québécois: "The Parti Québécois is strong; it is working to increase its importance in the opinion of the public; it is succeeding because it lets us hope for certain gains, although there are obvious economic risks. The Parti Québécois will stage a major electoral campaign in 1974, and they will make important gains, because they coincide with the desires of a large portion of the population—to control their own future. I doubt very much that Quebec will become totally independent because Canada—Ottawa—is very capable of opposing it by all political means, and even, if necessary, by force. Also as money speaks English, the Parti Québécois would not want to dispossess the English. I want independence, but by peaceful means."

I asked about the impact of the movement on the average French Canadian today. His right hand began to tremble, although he ap- had somehow touched some long-protected nerve, although he appeared unaware of it. "It is difficult to say. The next elections will inform us, by the percentage of votes received." What impact had it had on him personally? Until recently, Separatism had represented little more than a means of being conscious of history. As such, it had meant inner longing restrained by outer caution, "a risk, a battle lost before it was fought." As a student, he had been acutely aware of the lessons of 1837. "Independence as an idea we viewed with enthusiasm, but to us it was an idea with no possible chance of success." And now? "Now the movement is much stronger."

Although retired for nearly twenty years, Dion felt that the Parti Québécois had already been beneficial in economic terms. "It is a bit like a watchdog. They cannot take advantage of us. Yes, it does affect me, positively. The role, the position of the Parti Québécois forces the [provincial] government to control itself, and to adopt laws which are beneficial to the population." How else did it affect him, in economic terms? He may not have understood. "It keeps the population informed." How? "By means of conferences." I did not press the issue, sensing that he was tiring under the stress of the interview, and that I should move on to other questions. But in retrospect, and in context with the other answers, it seems that he meant, They cannot push us around any more, because we— French Canadians—know our rights. I personally benefit from the fact that other French Canadians know their rights. No longer will we give our unvoiced assent to economically injurious schemes, from which we all suffer. His response indicated a sophisticated recognition of the linkages between free communication and distribution of economic benefits. Would he, personally, gain more from supporting independence? He did not distinguish between himself and other French Canadians, nor between present and future benefits. "If it works, we all gain; if it does not work, we all lose."

He recalled becoming aware of the power potential of the movement in the years before World War I. "At the beginning of the twentieth century we perceived for the first time the possibilities of the nationalist movement. We were guided—by Henri Bourassa and *Le Devoir*—to the independence movement which exists today." This awareness was for him and others like him a source of power, usually incipient, but occasionally manifest, and for more than half a century he had resigned himself, like Milton, to stand and wait. He had been a subscriber to *Le Devoir* since the first issue; now, in the last years of his life he was witnessing the full power of Henri Bourassa's ideas.

Did the movement represent something different to today's youth? He did not think so. In his youth, the idea of independence "existed simply as a dream." But to be a Quebecer nevertheless meant the same thing as it does today: "to be a Canadian whose language is French—and to be accepted as such anywhere in Canada, just as in the province of Quebec." This concern, he added, presaged the policy of bilingualism, of which, on a theoretical level, he approved. Practically, however, he could not accept it, for it left much to be desired, and "the law is not applied equally."

As an individual he felt that he had gained nothing in terms of power from the movement, although as a French Canadian, he had benefited very positively.

Had the movement brought greater respect to the average French Canadian? "Yes. The Quebecer feels proud enough to be himself and to insist on his rights." The immediate reference to self-respect suggested that he was speaking not of the average French Canadian but of himself, and the directness of the response indicated that this may have been for him the most important function of the independence movement. Which Canadians were most respected now? "All of them—they are generally respected more." By whom? "The population of Canada, as the result of the current Quebec movement." It became necessary to get an education—to take advantage of the opportunities. The average French Canadian's feelings about his own history and culture had evolved, he believed, as the result of increased information. Public opinion was generally more enlightened in recent years, as a result of radio and television, which the movement had succeeded in penetrating. He accepted my hypothesis that the movement had created greater bonds of loyalty and affection among French Canadians, but he could see no way that it had affected his health or well-being.

To Edgar Dion, to be a Separatist was synonymous with being "someone who is a Quebecer," while by contrast a federalist was "a Canadian who favors the present system." He did not distinguish between Francophone and Anglophone federalists, as though the former category did not exist. Would he consider himself a Separatist or a federalist? "Je sympathise avec tout le monde. Je suis Canadien de langue française; par conséquent je sympathise plus avec le Parti Québécois." (I sympathize with everyone. I am a Canadian whose language is French; consequently I sympathize more with the Parti Québécois.)

INTERVIEW 23: MARTIN BLAIN, SITE INSPECTOR

The interview took place in the office-apartment at a hydroelectric site in rural Quebec, about thirty miles north of Quebec City. Having little else to do on a Sunday afternoon, Martin Blain, site inspector, union leader, and *Péquiste* agreed to answer my questionnaire.

Martin Blain began work as a laborer. He has no degree, no vocational training. Eight years' experience in excavating and constructing hydroelectric power stations qualified him for the job he now holds. He is responsible for seeing that the terrain is properly prepared for construction and graded afterward. Because Hydro-Québec is a provincial corporation, Martin is a government employee. Union membership is compulsory, although the precise organization varies from one region to another. Martin is president of his local organization, which numbers between thirty and forty members. In that capacity he has invited *Péquistes* to speak at union meetings, but, except for canvassing for the party, he is not involved in political activities. He told me that he was unable to influence the ideas of others. He does not engage in even informal discussion of the political situation. Slight, pale, and almost scholarly-looking, he does not have the appearance of one who spends much of each working day out of doors. There is nothing persuasive about him. He answered my questionnaire in a curiously im-

personal manner, eyes averted, as if the answer were to be found
hovering in the air, where I might see it also. There was no attempt
to persuade. He spoke with difficulty, often with long pauses. It
was necessary for him to concentrate on the questions, but he did
not seem anxious to end the interview.

"Ils sont allés au fond de la chose!" (They have gone to the heart
of the matter.) The Separatist movement had raised the single,
most critical issue of Quebec's political existence; all others were
superficial. The exact extent of the Separatist movement was un-
known, since at that time there was a certain fear of being independent. Many feared economic hurdles, and did not wish to lose what
little security they had. However, the movement had become much
more "determined" in recent years, and undergone "a type of internal change." Any changes in the near future would depend on the
results of the next elections, and whether it became an official
opposition capable of influencing the politics of the majority. Independence was "about the best solution, the administration of our
own government, by ourselves. Two administrations cost twice as
much; bilingualism is costly, too." Independence would come after
the Parti Québécois came to power, when the party's ideologues
made independence known for what it was, and the people realized
what they could do. Martin disapproved of violence; that type of
revolution was "a bad trip." He would vote for the Parti Québécois.

The chief impact of Separatism had been to express new ideas
and to "make people value old ones." Certain good ideas had helped
French Canadian nationalism to develop; Martin could appreciate
this because his father was a member of the Union Nationale while
Martin was growing up. Others concerned changes in the government, and would be good if applied. For example, there would be
positive economic benefits if a unitary (i.e., independent) government were substituted for the provincial (i.e., federal) one. Maintaining a federal system was expensive and unnecessary.

Martin could think of no way in which the movement had helped
him economically. He could not say whether even the unions had
gained from the movement, but he did not think so. Neither did he
gain political power from the movement. He shrugged. Nothing
had changed; the problems had been avoided by the legislature.
However, the Parti Québécois was growing stronger. If people
would join it . . . He did not finish the sentence, but there was no
need to. He had indicated the root of the problem, as he saw it: a
federalist legislature could never come to terms with the problems
of French Canadian nationalism; any attempt to do so would avoid

the question of independence and be doomed form the start. The only solution was therefore an electoral victory for the Parti Québécois, and for the first time the Separatist movement had recognized this.

Were French Canadians more respected now, as a result of the movement? Pause. Perhaps a bit. By whom? Long pause. "By different companies, especially American companies. They respect our point of view; they adapt themselves to our region. They hire French[-speaking] administrators." The average French Canadian also had more self-respect because he was "more conscious of what he can do, and he has been able to express himself more in the last ten years." He could think of no way in which respect might have declined.

The average French Canadian's feelings about his history and culture had changed significantly, Martin thought. Old feelings about nationalism had been rekindled on a new hearth. "To form one's own country—that is the greatest change to have come of this idea." Public opinion was more developed, and there was more access to information, although it was difficult to say that the average French Canadian was better informed now, not so much as a result of joining the Parti Québécois as through being conscious of the movement. "Let us say that it makes one value his ideas. This in turn affects the government. They are pressured to respond. I suppose it is the result of the movement, being well informed. Being educated, that comes as your life unfolds [*le déroulement de la vie*]." He was no better educated as the result of Separatism, but he could say that he was better informed, through contact with the ideas of the movement.

What about affection? A pause, a long smile. "Now? I can't say exactly. I couldn't discuss it. I was at a party until three o'clock last night. The PQ is not well known. [Your question] makes me reflect on this . . . more on the next government and on the present one. It cannot be discussed." Evidently, Separatist views were less than welcome in his circle. As for health and well-being, "I get along."

To Martin Blain, a Separatist was a person for independence completely, one who sought to form a single government administered by his own people *(des hôtes mêmes)*. A federalist, by contrast, was "a person formed during a past era, who wants to keep the former structures." Federalist attitudes are already formed; they are conservative and resist change. If there was a Separatist ideology, it was "an amelioration of certain things," but for him,

Separatism was "a response to a problem—to be able to determine." The structures were still not finished; there was still hope.

The interview generated considerable stress, both for the interviewer and the respondent. Martin Blain spoke no English, and his French was heavily *Joual*. Although he could understand standard French, and occasionally read the daily newspapers, he was, if not unfamiliar with the concepts involved in the interview, unaccustomed to relating them in response to a question. It was necessary to rephrase many of them. His responses also showed an inability to relate them to this own life, and, although the communication during the interview became intense at times, he appeared to be a detached, somewhat passive individual who was chiefly involved with his job. Aside from perusing *Le Soleil* and *La Presse* "if somebody brings them in," he usually read manuals on electronics. He had read "some of the people" who had written on Separatism, but could cite no names. That afternoon he was reading a union manual.

What then had caused him to join the Parti Québécois? There appear to be two reasons. The first was the influence of his father, a nationalist who had voted first for the Union Nationale and later for the PQ. The second, more important reason is that somehow, something in the PQ had, despite his overall detachment, evoked an emotional response sufficient for Martin to reject the status quo (which was unusual in his apolitical, lower-class milieu). While his arguments reflect, in large measure, those of the PQ, what is significant is that he had assimilated some and not others. Of these, the most important was the acceptance of independence as the ultimate expression of nationalism ("the greatest change to have come of this idea"; "the heart of the matter"). This was supported by the economic argument that two levels of government were too costly, and by the contention that dealing with unsympathetic administrators resulted in frustration for the average Quebecer. Martin also accepted the primacy of independence as the sole means of having his ideas validated. Only through the movement, with its commitment to independence, could his own thoughts about, and reactions to, the present political situation have significance. Not only was an answer provided, but the frustrations which he and other French Canadians shared were given consensual validation.

It was an inescapable impression that to him the party provided an immediate means of comprehending an otherwise unfathomable social situation. Given his educational background, there was no other way to structure the social, political, and economic conditions that affected his life. Like most of his generation, he no longer attended Mass. Sermons could no longer insist that he accept the role of apostle or martyr here in return for reward in another life. The PQ not only offered a more realistic explanation of his condition, but promised rewards much sooner.

If the Parti Québécois continued the Church's role as *magistra*, though, it abruptly cast its members into a new role, that of a dissenting minority. The reward, even on earth, did not come easily. The price of accepting the PQ's explanation was high: it required discontent with the present social and political situation in return for a possible amelioration in the future. Those willing to accept the federalist (Liberal) explanation faced no such predicament: no such unhappiness was required of them, and if there were any serious problems to be solved, the chances of doing so were more immediate than either the Church or the PQ would lead one to believe.

Why, then, accept the PQ as opposed to the federalist solution? It must be understood that to join with the PQ is first and foremost an emotional response, of which some, but not all, are capable. Essentially, it means that two realities coincide, one internal, the other external. The internal reality represents the inescapable conviction held by many French Canadians that they are not masters of their own house politically, and are without an identity of their own internally, as the result of the present federal arrangement. The external reality is the ideology and platform of the PQ. When the two correspond, people join the party. At present, and until the PQ assembles enough seats to be a functioning opposition in the legislature, its strength will be directly proportionate to the degree of correspondence between the internal reality of the French Canadians and the external reality of its ideology and program.

INTERVIEW 25: PAUL MARTIN, BUSINESSMAN

Paul Martin is a middle-management executive for a large international corporation. He is fifty-one years old, the father of four children ranging in age from thirteen to twenty. He grew up in a well-to-do home in Montreal. When he was twelve his mother died, and he was sent away to boarding school and subsequently went to

Georgetown University in Washington, D.C. He is thus fully bilingual, and speaks English with only a trace of an accent.

The interview took place late in the evening at Paul's home, a rented duplex apartment about twenty miles from Quebec. His wife, Noelle, remained upstairs. Paul explained that she would have been happy to meet me, but that as a government employee (she was an official translator for the provincial government) she was afraid of implicating herself by being present at the interview. She did not even say hello.

Although he had readily agreed to the interview, it appeared that Paul had had second thoughts about it. The interview lasted over three hours. It was entirely unlike any of the other interviews. Paul was relaxed, voluble, but evasive. He seemed consciously to resist expressing his own feelings about Separatism; at times he was almost flirtatious. After an hour he said, teasingly, "You'll never find out anything about me." I did not attempt to overcome this resistance, but continued to ask questions in the areas where he felt comfortable, gradually enlarging on these. By the end of the interview, this technique (together with the lateness of the hour) had succeeded sufficiently to give a clear picture of the way Separatism functions in Paul's life.

I began by asking Paul whether he ever discussed politics with friends. "We discuss sex. . . . We're so frustrated, that's about all we can discuss." Paul's political frustration, which became increasingly evident during the interview, was the product of identification with (and admiration for) Americans and English-speaking Canadians, and his awareness that he will always be, to himself and to them as well, a French Canadian. It was expressed repeatedly, at first through evasion of personal questions and long digressions, and later through an almost pathetic description of his own position between the two cultures. The following exchange indicates the degree to which this conflict affected his self-respect.

I asked whether he felt he had gained any respect as a result of the movement. He answered in a characteristically indirect, but revealing, manner. One of his colleagues, an English-speaking Canadian, asked him a question about the FLQ, which irritated him. "I said to him, 'I'm so goddam fed up personally with living in this country. I wish I could live in the States or Spain or anywhere else where I would never hear the difference between a Can[uck]²— a French Canadian and an English Canadian. I've been hearing that since I'm that high. My father, he's always been pro-American, or pro-English, and anything the French Canadians did, they were stupid, they were dumb, they were this, they were that, and of course, if I [went] somewhere else, I used to hear about the English, they were bastards . . . you know, you have a head like this at times." He made a gesture indicating a throbbing sensation.

Paul saw himself as an average French Canadian with the dubious advantage of having been taught to emulate the ruling class. "I don't think I'm an exception. I've been trained so many years. I'm used to work[ing] with [the] English-speaking. . . . We always learned to be efficient, we always learned the word efficiency, we always learned the word of responsibility, control, organization, you know, organize your work, plan your work. I'm so accustomed to this, it's second nature now.

"I would never work for any goddam French Canadian in my life. . . . I think they're a bunch of bastards. Sure. In business? They're the worst type of manager you could work for. . . . They have no business ethic, as far as I'm concerned." I asked him why. "They don't know what business is. . . . Does it mean business is to screw someone else?" He could offer neither sympathy nor explanation for this stereotype.

Because of his attempt to assimilate English values, Separatist demonstrations embarrassed him, and he used denial to avoid taking a stand. He recalled a riot in Montreal. "I said [to myself] it's not a nation, it's just maybe a group of five, ten men who are exercising some kind of power."

Paul is resigned to this perpetual conflict of identity, but he is nevertheless aware of it. His son Pierre is a *Péquiste*. And there is considerable exchange between the two. His elder son is a Marxist, and it is possible that alienation is discussed. Paul is also aware that his education has been a hindrance to him in developing an identity as a French Canadian, and even in forming an opinion as to whether he would prefer to live under a Quebec regime or a Canadian regime, but he had been sufficiently decisive to vote for the PQ in the 1970 election, and planned to do so again.

Trudeau's policy of bilingualism had alleviated this conflict considerably. Paul took this as an indication of increased respect, because "the English don't spend money unless they consider it important." He felt this was one of the greatest contributions of the Parti Québécois: it "has forced the other party to be on their toes regarding the French language"—and that these reforms might never have taken place had the PQ not kept the language issue in the foreground. The Union Nationale never applied pressure on the language issue.

If the federal policy of bilingualism was an indication of increased respect—which he valued—it was by no means a total solution for the conflict of identity. For Paul, this conflict could be overcome only by a solid identification as a Quebecer. I asked him what it meant to be Quebecer. "I will tell you this," he replied. "I think that the Jewish people, they have found their identity, their own country, and I think the French Canadians, that's what they need, really, apart from what may happen to them economically."

In contrast with many of the others interviewed, Paul did not feel that having his "own country" would require total separation. Separation could mean "separation of powers, separation of authority, of responsibility," or "more freedom for Quebec to operate, say, than the other provinces," or "the power to delegate their own ambassadors, without having real separation."

It became clear that Paul's conflict of identity and values was due chiefly to his absorbtion of the deprecating attitudes of the English-speaking Canadians with which he came into close and frequent contact. Paul thinks there is some basis for these attitudes; all the same, they are so painful for him that he is willing to accept a relatively radical solution, even if there is an economic disadvantage. This, he believes, will "save their pride" and ultimately enable them to work together.

Economically, Paul did not think he had gained anything as a result of the Parti Québécois. Like his wife, he could not express his approval too publicly, for fear of losing his job. However, one aspect of his employment has changed in a small but significant way: He is permitted to give courses for company personnel in French. This policy has changed only within the last few years; prior to that, all business had to be done exclusively in English. Paul thought that among many Canadians the fear of economic loss was an important restraint on the spread of Separatism. He likened the present relationship of Canadians and Quebecers to a marriage of convenience. Many more would be for separation if they felt that their economic security could be guaranteed.

Paul saw an increase in power in terms of "more respect and understanding" from the other side. He thinks this is the result of an increased pressure from Quebec and from the PQ. "If you stand up for your position, you always get more respect from your opponents." He believes that the Parti Québécois has done a great deal already toward forcing the other parties to deal with the issues of language and separatism. Essentially, he agrees with all their thinking, although he is not sure of what they will do in the key areas of welfare, education, and political power, to him, means the ability to deliver the two things most wanting in his life: respect and recognition of rights from the rest of Canada.

If the movement has brought Paul an increased awareness of his personal position, it has also served in his opinion to inform both federal and provincial governments of the need for change "especially regarding the French language."

Had the existence of Separatism brought him any more affection? He did not think it had, although his son Pierre had seemed extremely proud that his father was a *Péquiste*. Paul thought that it had brought respect, but not real affection. "Well, my boss, he's kissing me now, and speaking French. . . . I hate him when he tries to speak French, it bothers me, it's not natural!" He felt this display of affection was false, and it made him uneasy. "It's like trying to make love when you don't feel like it."

I did not have time to ask Paul how the movement had affected his health and well-being, but it was clear that there had been some benefit. It offers relief from the constant pressure of cultural conflict, of being a member of a minority culture unable to generate sufficient self-respect to offset the negative attitudes of the dominant one. Above all, the Separatist movement represents hope, a desperate hope that relations with Canada will change, and that even French Canadians will change—that with the independence will come self-knowledge, self-respect, and an increased sense of responsibility.

INTERVIEW 27: GEORGES CARON, SMALL BUSINESSMAN

Georges Caron spread out his fingers on the table before him, like a text to be read. Without looking up, he spoke insistently, rapidly. He is fifty-one years old, gray-haired, stocky. A member of the City Council of Ste.-Foy, he is an active member of the Parti Québécois, having twice been a candidate in provincial elections. His own political development has been characterized by the same stubborn independence as his business career. The thirteenth of sixteen children, Georges was the first in his family to have the opportunity for a secondary education. But he left high school in the second year, "in search of happiness." He did not settle down until he was twenty-six; by that time he had decided against seeking a university education because, as he still maintains, "men having access to a single source of information at the same time create a system." He did not need the astygmatism of such a system; instead, he began to think in a fashion "anarchic, a bit un-methodical, but to think by myself." In a successful career, first in banking and then as a stockbroker (with a specialty in municipal bonds), he developed his own theories about economics. His observations led him long ago to conclude that Quebec's economy can prosper only if the present federal system is replaced by a sovereignty-association.

The present relationship, he believes, has been detrimental to Quebec, with Ottawa draining her economically in an attempt to placate the western provinces. In a memorandum that he prepared in 1964, Caron argued that "the methods adopted by the minister of finance, Mr. Walter Gordon, for the assessment of expenditures and receipts by the Canadian government are like a phantom—that is, one which never materializes as an economic factor, either directly or indirectly, in the province to which it is arbitrarily assigned."[3] Although Quebec appears to contribute somewhat less than she receives from the federal government, this is hardly the case. The "benefits" computed by the federal government never reach Quebec.

The memorandum cites a number of examples. Subsidies for the transport of grain are calculated according to the destination of the cargo. This means that the transportation costs of grain exported by the western provinces are borne exclusively by the eastern ones, including Quebec. The costs of administering the deficit incurred in administering the St. Lawrence Seaway are calculated differently, but again to Quebec's detriment: this time, divided according to both origin and destination of traffic on the seaway. Georges Caron claims that since only the Welland Canal, which is entirely within the province of Ontario, operates at a deficit, the subsidy ought to be attributed entirely to Ontario. Other examples include expenditures calculated on a per habitant basis for all of Canada. "This method attributes to Quebec expenditures which have no link with reality."[4] In the case of National Defense, far less than the 28.84 percent of the budget attributed to Quebec is actually spent within the providence. Quebec's share of the national debt is also calculated according to population, at 28.84 percent, but only 24.3 percent of the interest is actually reinvested in the province.

Georges also told me that he felt the French Canadians were at a further disadvantage, under the present structure, because of their vastly different ways of doing business. The independent, nuclear, conservative method that prevails in Quebec cannot compete with the collective, peripheral, and venturesome corporations favored by the Anglo-Saxons. As a stockbroker, he greatly admires the technique and expertise of corporate enterprises, but as a French Canadian he is convinced that the political and economic structures must be changed, in order to promote the accumulation of wealth in Quebec. The present tax structure, he adds, tends to siphon off the profits of French Canadian business, while permitting large corporations to expand. "It is not in our chromosomes to take advantage of the corporation—or even a political party"; until the structures are changed, "French Canadians are incapable of 'taking off' economically."

It is quite possible that George's own 'takeoff' would be substantially helped, both economically and politically, by independence for Quebec. "I am not rich yet," he says. "When I take a vacation, I still use the same camper I bought six years ago." Perhaps his wider dreams have not yet materialized, but he attaches his trailer to a well-appointed, recent-model Cadillac. His own wealth has been acquired in the nuclear, conservative fashion he describes as typically French Canadian. In 1972 he invested money accumulated during his career as a stockbroker in what he feels is the fastest-growing industry in Quebec, tourism. A well-known restaurant in the heart of the tourist district was losing so much money that it was headed for bankruptcy. Its owners were anxious to sell it, together with several other properties in the same section of the city. When Caron heard about the possibility of acquiring these, he immediately began negotiations for a Howard Johnson's franchise, because he felt that substantial profits could be made from fast-food processing. At the same time, he set up a holding company. The franchise was granted in June of 1972, and he took title to the properties the same month. The restaurant was removed from its old quarters and integrated with a smaller one, bought at the same time, which was doing well. In its place is Howard Johnson's. "I was criticized for doing that," Caron says, "they called me a Separatist in collaboration with America . . . but I am a *Souverainist*. Sovereignty implies only a political option. It does not imply an economic option. I've always found that economics are international, whether it's . . . the Greeks running the restoration of the old city, or myself, running my business with the help of Americans—it doesn't matter because the profits are mine. And franchises, well, when a company has a quality of service or of a product which is well enough known to be franchised, so much the better for them.

"I do not turn up my nose at Americans. You can do business easily in English; you can't in French. It's not even funny. I love the language, and I've always appreciated it enormously. Myself, I've no animosity toward anyone, but I know [that without independence] we French Canadians will not be living well in the future, because we don't have the same way of life. We must be given our own governmental structures, and when we have been given [them], when we have acquired them, the foreman will have become the boss, as I've said all along. *Then* we'll begin to do business. That's why I've always been for association . . . because of the unfortunate international tendency to resist learning about things French Canadian. Just the same, I no longer consider myself French, not at all, I consider myself a Quebecer."

I asked him then what it meant to be a Quebecer, and his reply followed, long, involved, lacking in coherence at times, but nevertheless eloquent. His conception of what it is to be French Canadian is in the tradition of Groulx and Asselin,[5] since its emphasis is on innate aspects of character rather than collective experience. Yet for Georges Caron, the feeling of being a Quebecer developed as a result of personal experience. As a young man, he lived and worked in Ontario for short periods, before being drafted in World War II. At the beginning, he experienced it chiefly in terms of language. Later, while Quebec remained as a beacon in his consciousness, he became aware that Canada offered him a standard of living that surpassed most of Europe's. But "there was the problem of being French, quite simply."

Being "French," or French Canadian is a matter of consciousness based on territorial and familial identification. "When you have a number of persons who react in the same fashion, who feel at home only in the same place, then they are, sociologically speaking, in the process of becoming, of identifying, a country beneath their feet. When a country develops, one can say simply, it's my country because my father lived here, my friends lived here. It was the same thing for all the families that grew up—we identified under our feet the embryo of a country."

He feels that Quebec is already a nation, even though "it does not yet have all the forms of a nation." He points again to the distinct quality of life that, he feels, characterizes Quebec. "Here is emerging a whole generation of people, who have nearly. . . , for whom the dividend has no importance whatsoever. For them, their conception of life is consumption, but only because it is the first necessity. They enjoy living well, but on the other hand, they can pass it up, yes. . . . Now, we are not going to dig up everything simply to have more money, we are moving into a society which feels better. Perhaps Quebec is going to develop much more rapidly than the Americans . . . this idea of well-being and not riches, of well-being for all the people and not riches for the few and a bit of well-being for the others. Possibly we'll be glad to form that new society, which is, in a way, much more precise than yours. You others, you want to have a total structural revolution—to throw out—in order to arrive at a better social well-being for all individuals. We here have a system which costs us plenty . . . but where human beings have a tendency much more humane than you can be individually. . . . You Americans, you are very humane, but your structures are very cruel, just as you permit them. . . . We would not permit this, because a new generation is emerging which will accommodate itself [to necessary reforms].

    ". . . I've identified a special character in the Quebecer: he doesn't forget his sense of value. When you compare [him with] an Anglo-Saxon, he's always inferior [in economic terms]. But if you compare a man who has human qualities, if you wait . . . you have a difference. Because in the first stage, the Quebecer will be an introvert. But in the next stage of development, as a man, that will happen. He has the advantage of being Latin." This reference to a "Latin" heritage was repeated by other respondents. It is surprising in view of the fact that Quebec was colonized chiefly by emigrants from Normandy and other northern areas of France. It may be a reference to the Roman Catholicism which distinguished them from Anglo-Canadians. For Georges Caron, the Latin, Quebec identity represents a commitment to a "higher," more egalitarian value system than that adhered to by other Canadians, and the renunciation of the materialist, competitive system under which they have fared poorly. Independence will not require a total revolution, it will merely complete the structure Quebec needs for the protection of these values. Caron thinks that independence will come "very rapidly" if Trudeau is defeated, although he does not specify by what means.

    He does not think that he has either gained or lost anything, economically, although this is of little importance to him. What is important is to prove that Separatism is economically viable, even at the present state. "I bought a newspaper in order to prove that a Separatist press can survive in Quebec. In effect, I brought the *Journal de Ste.-Foy* to life." That was in 1970, when he ran for office as a *Péquiste*. Since then, he has sold approximately $10,000 worth of advertising per week.

Politically, he has gained something, although less than he had hoped for. What power he does have comes to him by an unusual but (in view of the dynamics of the situation) characteristically French Canadian route. "I'm known as a boy who's never compromised," he says. "I've never taken extreme positions, but when I have, I've never told anyone. They say in Quebec that I'm a reasonable man."

The respect he enjoys is thus an important element in the power he holds. He has earned this respect, he believes, because of the attention he has devoted to the study of economic aspects of the situation, and the originality and validity of his work. Much of his 1964 memorandum has now been incorporated by the Parti Québécois. He claims not to attach much importance to this respect; "Myself, I'm content because I've been faithful to my thinking, and let's say that personally, I'm happier, for example, in my relations with my family. . . . I don't think I'm a peacock!" He had difficulty in discussing self-respect, preferring to use the French term, *amour propre*. Separatism had brought its adherents "a pride in being souverainiste, . . . and above all, the wish that other French Canadians might become like all other peoples on earth, if they become a nation." He had the opinion the "French Canadians who are not Separatist lack pride."

It would seem that Georges Caron has earned this respect as a result of his need to be educated, in compensation for the years of schooling which he missed, and also as a result of his perception, while still a young man, that the existing social, political, and economic structure was in need of change. But has the movement brought him more information? "It's a difficult question. Let's say I'm an observer of all social situations—Canadian, North American, Quebec. I don't pretend to be better informed. You might say I'm better informed, you might say I've had enough [to do] not developing partisan politics for my idea of Sovereignty." Certainly, both he and the movement have profited from his studies.

He did not feel that he had experienced any greater loyalty as a result of Separatism. What was more important was to be "true to yourself." Loyalty and affection had profound sources and were rooted in a "national consciousness" which was still embryonic in

Quebec. Violence was one way of generating national consciousness, and it had been used already in Quebec. It had not succeeded,
he said, because it was unable to generate a collective consciousness
rapidly enough before being repressed. This consciousness would
therefore have to come from an improved self-respect and other
similar sources.

   Although Georges Caron is now a well-known public figure, in
many ways he is still representative of a majority of French Canadians. The interview is interesting because it took on the form of a
stream of consciousness: once he had said all that he planned to say,
a high degree of spontaneity emerged. This spontaneity combined
with his volubility to produce a rich monologue, drawing its material from those wells and sources which he shares in common with
other French Canadians. His frequent references to inherent differences between Quebecers and other Canadians were most striking.
Experience, both collective and individual, was relatively unimportant in his ideas about the French Canadian nation. He is therefore—and perhaps because of his age—far more influenced by the
nationalism of the 1930s than by the Separatism of the Parti
Québécois.

INTERVIEW 28: CONVERSATION IN A SWIMMING POOL WITH TWO TWELVE-YEAR-OLD BOYS

AG: May I ask you a question?
TWO BOYS: Yes.
AG: Do you think that Quebec will be independent one day?
DARK-HAIRED BOY: I don't think about it.
BLOND BOY *with scuba mask, teeth chattering:* Yes.
AG: Why?
BLOND BOY *with teeth chattering:* Because then they will tell the truth
   more.
AG: How?
BLOND BOY: They will no longer be able to lie to us in Quebec.
AG: Who?
BLOND BOY: The government.
AG: In Quebec?
BLOND BOY: No.
AG: In Ottawa?

BLOND BOY: Yes. (At this point he begins to shake uncontrollably, and dives under the water)

AG: How old are you?
BOTH: Twelve.
AG: Do you both live in Quebec?
(Simultaneously) DARK-HAIRED BOY: Yes.
                   BLOND BOY *with scuba mask:* Yes.
DARK-HAIRED BOY: Are you from Quebec?
AG: No . . .
DARK-HAIRED BOY: From Montreal?
AG: No, from New York.
DARK-HAIRED BOY: You've come a long way in order to swim.
AG: Yes, but I'm not only swimming. I'm writing a book about peoples' ideas about independence for Quebec. I was just wondering what young people thought.
BOTH: Oh. (They swim away).

DARK-HAIRED BOY *(treading water):* What is the title of your book?
AG: It's on the idea of independence in Quebec.
BOY: You're at the beginning?
AG: I don't understand.
BOY: Have you started writing?
AG: Yes.
BOY: How much?
AG: Oh, just some historical material. Like Papineau and the insurrection of 1837. (Blank stare.) Yesterday or the day before I was talking with an old man, eighty-three years old, who has always wished for independence. But they always feared it, because of what happened to Papineau. (Blank stare. He is now treading water, and gradually his feet float forward and he moves backwards, toward the opposite ladder).

BLOND BOY, *scuba mask on top of head now:* Have you any more questions for us?
AG: Yes. Do you often discuss politics at home?
BOTH: Yes, yes.
AG: Have you heard of the *Péquistes?*
BOTH: Yes.
AG: Do you think it's a good thing?
BOTH: Yes.

BLOND BOY: Do you have any more questions to ask us?

AG: No, but I'll be back as soon as I think of one. One more question for you. If Quebec becomes independent, to what extent will it be independent?

BLOND BOY: *Complètement.*

AG: Really?

BLOND BOY: Yes, *complètement.*

AG: Do you think that's good?

BLOND BOY: Perhaps, yes.

AG: You say you discuss politics at home. But your parents must be of the professional class.

BLOND BOY: Yes.

AG: Do other children—the children of workers, for example—discuss politics?

BLOND BOY: They don't talk about anything.

INTERVIEW 24: JEANNE NADEAU, HOUSEWIFE AND FEDERALIST

At twenty-eight, Jeanne Nadeau is chiefly concerned with the care of her two children, Jeanne-Françoise, six, and Clément-François, four and a half, and with her household, which she manages with deliberate style. She and her husband, Guy, take their upper-middle-class life-style seriously, more as an obligation than as a privilege. Small things, such as borrowing wineglasses for a country supper, are important to her. The wife of a home-furnishings-company executive, she is consumption-oriented. She has never worked, although she holds a degree in mathematics from Laval and is a member of a professional mathematicians' association. She hopes to get a job in a year or two. Jeanne and her sister grew up in a comfortable home in Quebec. She feels at home there. She has traveled extensively in Europe, but does not like Montreal, where, she feels, the people are unpleasant and "have no culture." She is committed to Quebec, but to a region and standard of living that are familiar.

Jeanne was my neighbor at a resort village in the Laurentians where she spends two months each summer. She rarely played with the children. Most of the time they were watched by her mother. I sometimes spoke with Jeanne on the lawn that connected our vacation houses. She was articulate without being intellectual, and consented eagerly to answering my questionnaire.

We sat on the glider, one of several pieces of lawn furniture she had brought from Quebec. She was apprehensive about putting the interview on tape, and I therefore recorded her answers on the questionnaire. She was surprised that I wrote them in French, and when I questioned her about this, she replied anxiously, "You are writing exactly what I am saying! Please do not tell my name!" She had not expected to be quoted when she consented to the questionnaire. Although she reads *Le Soleil* daily, and *Le Devoir* occasionally, Jeanne had never considered most of the questions as presented in the questionnaire. Her answers were, it seemed, extremely candid, guarded only by her understandable hope that her future would be as pleasant and secure as her present.

Jeanne does not know many Separatists now, although she did have a few Separatist friends at the university. Her knowledge of the movement is based chiefly on what she reads in the two newspapers mentioned, "a book published by the Parti Québécois," the name of which she could not remember, and from "fairly frequent" discussions with her friends. Independence is also a topic of conversation within the family, but under no circumstances does she try to persuade anyone, feeling it "more important to respect their views." Jeanne and Guy are hesitant about expressing a strongly federalist point of view with new acquaintances. I felt that they considered the discussion of politics a requisite of their upper-middle-class life-style, rather than an urgent personal concern. Except for voting—for the Liberal party—in federal and provincial elections, they take no part in politics. Thus, although in terms of affluence and education they are in the minority, in terms of real politicization, they are still members of the majority.

Jeanne felt that the movement had definitely "moved forward in the last twelve years," and that it was "stronger than it had been." It was calmer now than two or three years ago, which was a normal process, since with success it had tended to stabilize itself, and people were "better informed." Within the next five years, she felt, the Separatists would get more seats in Parliament, but at the same time people would become more fearful of the consequences of being a country themselves, and so the movement would tend to temper itself. Jeanne thought Quebec would become independent one day, but "not for fifteen or twenty years—at *least* twenty, because before that happens [the movement] will have to increase in power." She hoped that it would be only a "political" independence, because she was afraid of a complete break with Canada. "Political" independence would enable Quebec to take care of her own needs and would require Ottawa to concede more and more rights. How did she feel about independence? "Political independence is not [complete] independence," and she felt that she might be able to accept it.

Despite her reservations about the outcome of the movement, Jeanne felt that its existence had been beneficial. "It has brought us to the realization that we have rights, and that they cannot take advantage of us. There is less unhappiness now." What rights had the movement implemented? "The right to French culture and the use of French as a *langue de travail* [working language]." She felt this to be a more problem for Quebec than for Ottawa, but was generally pleased with Trudeau's handling of the problem, believing that he was able to present it to the rest of Canada, to Quebec's advantage. There was also the problem of taxation and revenue sharing, and of foreign capital; here, she thought, the opinions of Quebec were better understood throughout Canada. Just how the Separatist movement had enabled a Liberal prime minister better to represent the interests of Quebec, she did not specify. When asked how these advantages had been realized, she replied, "The movement has opened our eyes to the fact that in Ottawa they do not bother to consult us, and they do not respect us."

Jeanne was totally unaware that she had starkly contradicted herself. On the one hand, she asserted that the most important issue facing Quebec, that of language, could best be dealt with by the province; on the other, she indicated that the solution was to be provided in Ottawa. Even more significant was the contradiction between her statement that a great deal more esteem had been forthcoming from Ottawa in recent years, and her assertion that "in Ottawa they do not bother to consult us, and they do not respect us." A possible explanation is that Jeanne was merely expressing some of the inherent contradictions of a complex situation. However, her total unawareness of this conflict and her failure to synthesize or even explain it appear to indicate a more basic indecision, a failure to come to terms with what she expects from federalism and what it can provide.

Economically, Jeanne thought that the movement had been of substantial benefit to herself, her family and Quebecers in general. Her husband's company was a French Canadian corporation, and was expanding and doing well. "The movement can have a positive effect because the people—the mass of the population—it touches them. They spend their money in Quebec. They buy their furniture from a Quebec-owned company." The province was enjoying an unprecedented prosperity, she felt, because people were more aware of the importance of keeping profits in Quebec; also, their feelings about themselves had improved to the point where they no longer felt their environment was improved by patronizing Anglo-Canadian establishments or by purchasing Anglo-Canadian or American goods.

As far as power was concerned, Jeanne said, the movement had had no discernable effect on her own life, since she was occupied mainly as a housewife and mother and did not belong to any political organizations. If she worked outside the home, perhaps it might, but not now. However, she was quite emphatic in saying that the movement did not leave her with less power. Did the existence of Separatism give more power to any organization she could think of? "Yes, the cooperative [retailing] movement, but not political power—it doesn't touch politics—but it is formulating a manifesto on the rights of the consumer." Politically, there were a "good many federalists" who were benefitting from the independence movement, but she was not among them. There was only one current political effect that she could discern, and that was a vague feeling that "we are better administered by ourselves, and that we are better heard on the federal level."

The movement had definitely brought greater respect to the average French Canadian, although there were still other Canadians who seemed to differ with their opinions. But "if there has been an amelioration it is all of French Canada that benefits, not only the Separatists." Within Quebec, there was a greater sense of belonging to a national entity and the *fierté d'appartenance* (pride in belonging) that so many experienced. No, she could not think of any French Canadians who were less respected now, but of course that depended on what party they belonged to. Federalists would naturally be more respected by other federalists, while Separatists would be more respected by Separatists. These divisions did exist, after all, and one stood to lose friends by switching sides. If one's friends were federalist, one would be less respected for having Separatist views. I mentioned that I had spoken with Claude Morin several days before. Although she knew all about his politics,[6] she was impressed. "He is still very much respected. He arrived at his decision gradually." Obviously Claude Morin had not lost the respect of all federalists.

Jeanne felt that she had neither lost nor gained respect as the result of the movement. She claimed not to care about respect from other Canadians, and it is quite possible that her status as an affluent, educated housewife afforded her a certain immunity to the scornful attitudes of other provinces. Her life, if not deeply challenging, was pleasant, varied, and extremely satisfying in terms of the luxuries available to her and freedom from anxiety about financial matters. What was more important to her, it seemed, was the approval of her friends and her husband's colleagues. Insulated as she was by her daily life, she could not do without this source of external approval.

During the weeks that I knew Jeanne, we had many informal conversations. We always had difficulty distinguishing between "the average French Canadian" and "the cultivated class," as she put it. We could never agree on precisely where the line should be drawn. To her, affluence and education placed one squarely in the "cultivated class," which she also referred to as the "upper," or "professional" class. When I told her that in the States a person with an income of $40,000 a year would be considered affluent, and might be a professional, but would certainly not be considered upper class unless his income was derived from invested wealth, she was incredulous. She had never considered the possibility that there might be an entire stratum of society whose affluence was not based on earned income, or that there might be more important continuities between the lower- and upper-middle-class than between the upper-middle and leisure class. Part of the difficulty, I later decided, was due to a need and determination to distinguish herself and her family from the mass of French Canadians. Since she was not in a position to distinguish herself professionally (i.e., as a mathematician), she did so through the time-honored device of snobbery. There was also the factor that in Quebec, at least among the French Canadians, there has never been a leisure class. Historically, this role was filled by the clergy, and, since this estate was rigidly defined, there was no possibility of falsely identifying oneself as a member of it. Although there are now a few families with inherited wealth, they by no means constitute a class. It is thus quite easy to see how someone seeking a basis for self-esteem might attempt to distinguish herself from the lower echelons of society by referring to herself as "cultivated," "professional," or "upper class." Without an existing leisure class to challenge her own status, it does not seem entirely unrealistic of Jeanne to place herself in the upper stratum of society. What is significant here is that in emphasizing the importance of class and in identifying with this particular stratum, Jeanne was tacitly rejecting national unity. Unwittingly, she had chosen horizontal linkages over vertical ones. For her, self-

4. Ibid., p. 10.

5. Canon Lionel Groulx became the spokesman for the reactionary nationalist movement that emerged after 1900 and reached its peak in the 1920s and 1930s.

6. Claude Morin, a former deputy minister and influential member of the Liberal party, had resigned his position and joined the PQ a few months earlier. He was then preparing to run for election to the Provincial legislature as a *Péquiste*. See below, p. 0.

7. Marcelle Dolment and Marcel Barthe, *La Femme au Québec* (Montreal: Les Presses libres, 1973), pp. 13–14.

Part 3
Six Functions of Separatism

5 • Parameters

The case studies, together with the results of the November 1976 election, make it apparent that Separatism sustains itself not because of the appeal of the movement's specific goals, but because of the way in which it addresses the needs, both conscious and unconscious, of individuals. No two people benefit from it in exactly the same way: each possesses a unique value process, and the specific gains and their interrelations vary accordingly. An in-depth analysis of each person's total process of needs and values was not feasible. What has been undertaken here is an analysis of the way in which Separatism, as an independent variable, satisfies his apparent needs. Part 2 attempted to describe this process on an individual basis; the present chapter will deal with the problem collectively. In its broadest sense, Separatism is a constellation of attitudes regarding the independence of Quebec. The functions of this attitude constellation in satisfying the needs of those individuals who were interviewed for this study will be the subject of the present chapter.[1] These functions will be referred to as *value functions*.

Thus *(Proposition 1)* Separatism (attitude constellation S) gives to each individual (respondent I) a given amount (n) of the values Power (P), Wealth (W), Respect (R), Enlightenment (E), Affection (A), and Health and Well-being (HW):

$$S \text{ gives } I \quad \begin{array}{l} n\,P \\ n\,W \\ n\,R \\ n\,E \\ n\,A \\ n\,HW \end{array}$$

Or, $n\,P$, $n\,W$, $n\,R$, $n\,E$, $n\,A$ and $n\,HW$ are value functions of S. If we review the results of all the interviews with Separatists, the following composite emerges:

	P	W	R	E	A	HW
	n =	n =	n =	n =	n =	n =
I 7 (Priest)	5	1	4	5	5	5
I 11 (2 Revolutionaries)	4	1	4	5	3	3
I 12 (Teacher)	4	4	5	5	5	5
I 15 (Salesman)	4	3	4	4	4	4
I 17 (Waitress)	3	3	2	4	2	4
I 18 (Bureaucrat)	2	2	5	5	4	5
I 19 (Mechanic)	5	4	5	5	5	5
I 20 (Politician)	4	3	5	5	3	5
I 21 (Student)	4	3	4	4	4	4
I 22 (Retired person)	4	4	5	5	4	4
I 23 (Site Inspector)	3	3	4	4	2	4
I 25 (Businessman)	4	4	4	4	4	4
I 27 (Small businessman)	5	5	5	5	5	5
I 28 (Boys in pool)	3	3	4	4	n.a.	5
	3.85	3.07	4.28	4.57	3.84	4.42

Table 1

The amounts of values *P* through *HW* are represented on a 1 to 5 scale, with 1 indicating a significant loss, 2 a perceptible loss, 3 neither a perceptible loss nor a perceptible gain, 4 a perceptible gain, and 5 a significant gain. These amounts refer to the individuals' net loss or gain as a result of the existence of Separatism.

One glance at Table 1 tells us how uniquely Separatism functions for each individual. If we read across, no two lines are alike. Yet if we read downward, it becomes clear that, generally speaking, certain benefits are more substantial than others. The average amount of Enlightenment gained was substantial ($n = 4.57$). The economic gains, however, were meager, with n averaging only 3.07. In between, in declining order, were Health and Well-being ($n = 4.42$), Respect ($n = 4.28$), Power ($n = 3.85$) and Affection ($n = 3.84$).

These figures give some indication of the direction and intensity of the Separatist appeal; at the same time they tell us something about Separatism and the value structure within which it functions. Basically, the Separatists interviewed tended to accept a more specifically French Canadian value structure than did their federalist counterparts. This structure, which has been described in part 1, has three main features that correspond with the findings here.

The first feature that can be identified is the willingness to compromise with Power. Most of the Separatists did not especially care about having power, either personally or collectively, despite the insistence of party officials that the PQ must significantly increase its appeal if the movement is to survive. Paradoxically, it was this traditional ideology of survival—this ability to sublimate the need for power in order to enjoy other values—which both sustained and limited the Separatist movement. It sustained it in the sense that the PQ's poor showing in the 1970 and 1973 elections did not inhibit its phenomenal growth in the eight years following its inception; it limited it in the sense that those who were unable to sublimate this need for political power found themselves rejecting the traditional ideology and embracing the federalism of the Liberal party. The relatively low intensity recorded for Power reflects this tendency; it would also seem to indicate that power, as an end in itself, is not what compels people to become Separatist. Conversely, people who care very much about having immediate power will not usually be attracted to Separatism, in its early phases.

Separatists also exhibited a tendency to sublimate the need for Wealth. The tradition that promised future rewards in return for present hardships appears to have survived in the Separatist movement. The low intensity (3.07) of this function would indicate that Wealth was even less significant than Power in inducing people to become Separatist, and that those who were interested in having immediate Wealth would be more attracted to an ideology that emphasized, or was at least compatible with this value. Thus, most of the federalists interviewed said that they benefited substantially from economic integration with the rest of Canada and dismissed Separatism as economically unsound and potentially disastrous. Separatists, on the other hand, argued that the economic benefits were secondary in importance to the issue of national and cultural survival, and that economic viability, at the very least, could be achieved without compromising French Canadian survival.

The third general aspect of this value structure is its emphasis on self-knowledge and self-respect. The isolation of French Canadians on a largely Protestant, English-speaking continent made it all the more necessary that these values be defined within their own society and in their own terms. By drawing distinctions between themselves and others it was possible to reaffirm the value of their traditions and culture, and their own worth as well. Traditionally, French Canadians have felt that the Canadian experience had little, if any, meaning for them. They could learn nothing about themselves from it, and they could see in it no universal values by which to judge themselves. The collective experience brought neither knowledge nor self-respect; the national experience brought both of these. For this reason, many French Canadians have rejected as meaningless any collective Canadian experience as well as all attempts at integration. They thus appropriate for themselves the task of structuring and defining an "alternative" experience and set of values.

Federalists, on the other hand, appear to function in a different universe. They generally believed in a Canadian experience, and tended to reject Separatism not only because it did not offer them what they wanted, but because they considered it parochial. In varying degrees, their identity and values were defined by their Canadian experience. While it was apparent that most of them gained something from Separatism, they were so much more conscious of what they got from federalism that there was little chance of their changing position. Separatism was simply not functional in their lives, chiefly because they could not perceive it as such. Thus, despite the intensity of the Separatist pull, its functions were limited to a minority of French Canadians. Although the Parti Québécois has since come to power, there is no major function that it performs that appears capable of making as significant a contribution in the lives of federalists. Interviews showed that federalists were benefiting substantially from supporting federalism and that they regarded themselves as gaining far more from federalism than Separatists were gaining from Separatism. The interviews with federalists appear to indicate that the functions of Separatism were limited to a sector of the population that structured the political dilemma in terms of traditional values. These individuals responded to Separatism because there was little likelihood, given their life situations and outlook, that they would have gained anything from federalism. Separatism, at least, provided them with a set of values around which they could structure or restructure their lives.

Thus far this analysis has focused on the relative intensity of each of the functions of Separatism. But intensity is less significant than the way in which each value is enjoyed or the ways in which they interrelate. Power, Wealth, Respect, Enlightenment, Affection, and Health and Well-being will therefore be discussed in terms of two additional parameters, *mode* and *facilitation*. How does Separatism bring more respect? Why? *Intensity* has already been employed to indicate the degree of respect an individual gains; for example, a politician may experience a significant amount of respect as a result of leaving the Liberal party and joining the Parti Québécois, even though it means giving up a responsible position in the bureaucracy. *Mode* is the form in which a value is enjoyed; in this case he experiences respect chiefly as *mentorship*. Finally, *facilitation* is a term used here to indicate the main source of support in the enjoyment of a given value.[2] The politician in question enjoys a very significant amount of Respect, and he experiences it chiefly because he is known to have thought long and hard about his decision and arrived at it gradually.[3] Respect, in this case, is facilitated by the value, Enlightenment. Two other parameters remain more or less constant throughout, and are therefore given more cursory attention. Domain, or the number of individuals involved, is limited in direct reference to those interviewed. When reference is made to the substantial minority that they represent, it will be clearly indicated. Since the main purpose of the interview was to focus on the *immediate* effects of Separatism, *duration* was not specifically measured by the questionnaire. Thus, unless indicated otherwise, this study deals with the functions of Separatism in the four-month period immediately preceding the October 1973 provincial election. The concept of Weight is, I feel, more appropriately replaced by the parameters of *intensity* and *facilitation*, since the main focus of this study is to examine the function of Separatism, in terms of symbolic values, for a given number of individuals, rather than to weigh the success of Separatist policy. Facilitation is an especially useful concept because it provides a means for assessing the number and variety of functions for each symbolic value.

NOTES————————————————————————

1. A total of 23 individuals gave sufficiently complete responses for the results to be tabulated. Of these, 16 were pro-independence. In two cases, two persons were interviewed simultaneously, and their responses were consolidated. There are thus 14 "separatist" encounters.

2. Lasswell and Kaplan, *Power and Society*, p. 7. Facilitation is defined here as "support among acts." In this dissertation, the concept is used in an expanded sense, to include support among internalized responses.

3. This view was also expressed by both Jeanne Nadeau and her husband, but it appeared to be widely held.

6 • Paradigms

The *G* paradigm of symbolic values (Fig. 1) provides an ideal framework for recording the specific functions of Separatism in satisfying the needs of the persons interviewed. It makes it possible to record graphically the unique function of Separatism for each individual, and it has further merit in that it is sufficiently formal to permit quantification and tabulation of current data. The *G* paradigm represents a system of the six basic values, all of which are capable, hypothetically, of supporting others. The six values are designated by points on the perimeter of the structure, with lines connecting each point with the five others:

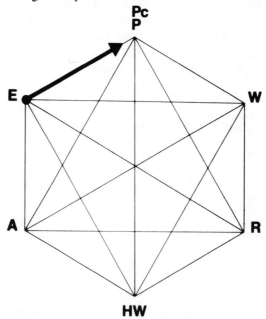

Fig. 1. The basic paradigm of value facilitation, showing one hypothetical demonstrable facilitation of Power through Enlightenment.

Each line represents a possible source of support. In this analysis, the primary source of support is represented by a black line between two functions. In the four instances where the facilitative relationship is not current but anticipated, a dotted line [...............] is used. Where there is conflict rather than facilitation, a series of vertical lines [| | | | | | | | | | | |] is utilized to indicate the one value which is most detrimental to the enjoyment of the other. In several of the cases studied, there was a clear distinction to be made between personal and collective power. Where the enjoyment of a given value (in all of the cases recorded, Enlightenment) was clearly facilitated by collective rather than personal power, this is indicated by the addition of point Pc directly above point P, and the line of facilitation is drawn from point Pc.

The G paradigm is a useful device for recording the functions of Separatism (or any other variable) since the specific patterns of one or more individuals may be superimposed. The superimposition of all the patterns results in a specific "Separatist" profile that, even if representative only of the sixteen persons interviewed, can be explained nevertheless in terms of Quebec's history and culture.

Figures 2 through 15 indicate the process by which the six value functions interact for each individual. For example, Sebastian Dupré (I_7, Fig. 2) experienced Power as a result of the Respect earned by his outspoken advocacy of Separatism. This Respect was facilitated primarily by Enlightenment: Sebastian was respected because of his intellectual commitment to the movement. This commitment also brought him Affection from others who were similarly committed. Affection, in turn, contributed greatly to his sense of Well-being, and this emotional stability made it possible for him to focus his attention on the issues of Separatism. On the other hand, his intellectual commitments have negatively affected the material comforts which he enjoys.

These patterns represent graphically the interaction of the six value functions of Separatism for each individual. Two pattern types may be identified: focused patterns and diffuse patterns. In the focused patterns, a single value function facilitates at least three of the five others. Stated another way, for certain individuals the benefits to be had from Separatism are contingent upon the enjoyment of one particular value or the satisfaction of one main need. Respondents whose value patterns were focused in this way included two revolutionaries (I_{11}), Roger, the salesman (I_{15}), Claude Morin, the politician and university professor (I_{20}), Pierre, a student (I_{21}), Martin Blain, the site inspector (I_{23}) and Paul Martin, the

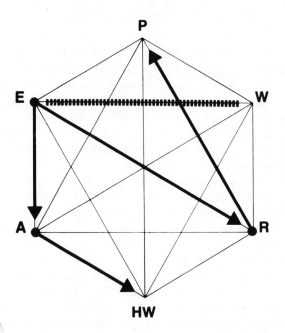

Fig. 2. Value Pattern I_7 *(Priest)*

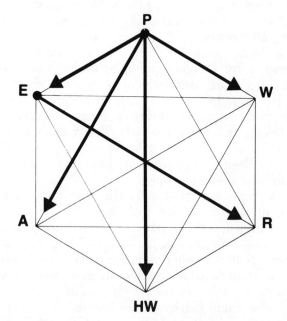

Fig. 3. Value Pattern I_{11} *(Revolutionaries)*

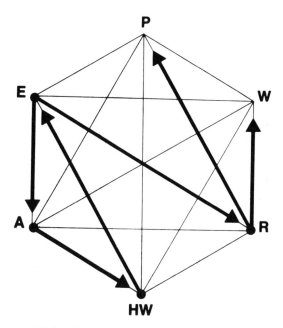

Fig. 4. Value Pattern I_{12} *(Teacher)*

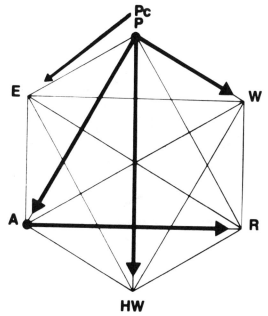

Fig. 5. Value Pattern I_{15} *(Salesman)*

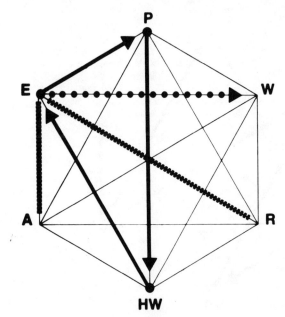

Fig. 6. Value Pattern I_{17} *(Waitress)*

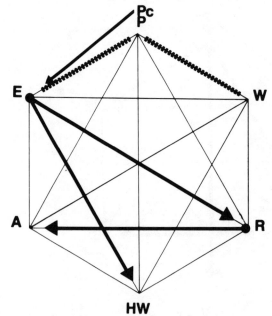

Fig. 7. Value Pattern I_{18} *(Bureaucrat)*

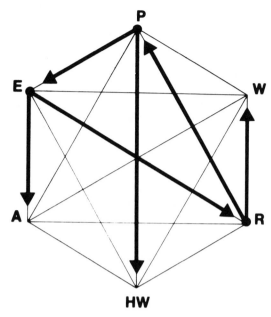

Fig. 8. Value Pattern I_{19} *(Mechanic)*

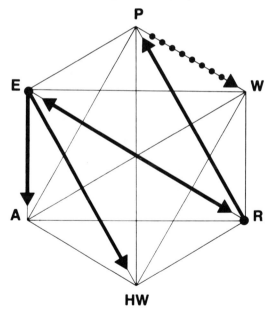

Fig. 9. Value Pattern I_{20} *(Politician and Professor)*

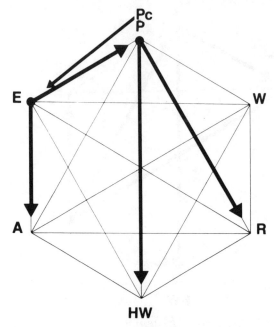

Fig. 10. Value Pattern I_{21} (Student)

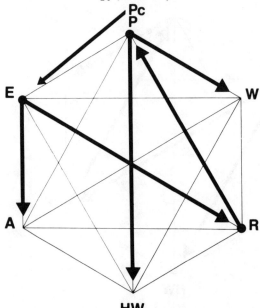

Fig. 11. Value Pattern I_{22} (Retired Person)

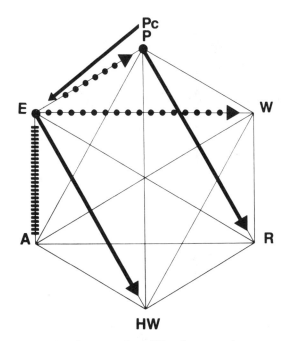

Fig. 12. Value Pattern I₂₃ *(Site Inspector)*

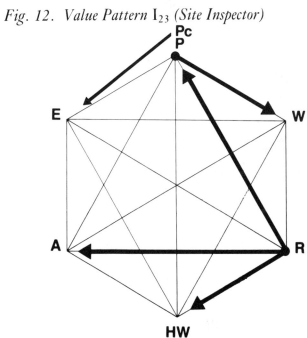

Fig. 13. Value Pattern I₂₅ *(Businessman)*

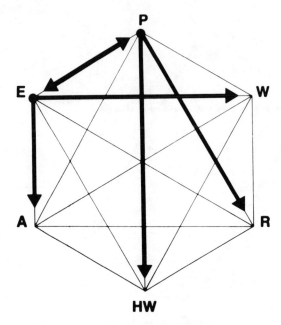

Fig. 14. Value Pattern I_{27} *(Small Businessman)*

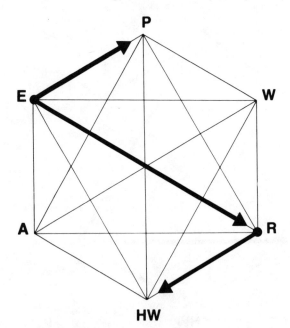

Fig. 15. Value Pattern I_{28} *(Boys in Pool) (incomplete)*

businessman (I_{25}). The value functions that had multiple facilitations of this kind were Power (in three instances), Enlightenment (in two), and Respect (in one). While the sample is too small to support any formal hypothesis relating the degree of focus and intensity of commitment, the proposition that those persons whose value patterns are sharply focused tend to be less committed to Separatism is worth considering. Persons with diffuse value patterns—those whose satisfaction was facilitated by a variety of value functions—appeared to have a deeper and less tenuous commitment to Separatism. These persons included Sebastian Dupré, Jacques Roche, the teacher (I_{12}), Hélène, a waitress (I_{17}), Philippe Beauséjour, the bureaucrat (I_{10}), Jean Dupont, the mechanic (I_{19}), Edgar Dion, the retired chemist (I_{22}), Georges Caron, the small businessman (I_{28}) and the two twelve-year-old boys in the pool (I_{28}).

Also worth noting is the fact that certain values tend to be more highly facilitative than others. Not only are Power, Enlightenment, and Respect the main foci of value patterns I_{11}, I_{15}, I_{20}, I_{21}, I_{23} and I_{25}, but they are highly facilitative in the diffuse patterns as well. Power, Enlightenment, and Respect are the values that made the greatest difference in peoples' lives. These value functions, then, were the chief means by which Separatism sustained itself in the period before 1976.

Although no two of the fourteen value patterns are alike, certain elements, such as $E \rightarrow R$ and $Pc \rightarrow E$ do tend to be repeated, and one repeated configuration,

$$E \rightarrow A$$
$$E \rightarrow R$$
$$R \rightarrow P$$

can be observed in figures 2, 4, 8, 9, and 11; in figures 2 and 4 this configuration also includes $A \rightarrow HW$ and $HW \rightarrow E$, so that they are nearly identical. There is every reason to believe that a larger sample would reveal a higher incidence of repeated configurations and even repeated patterns. It should be noted, also, that the configurations and patterns presented in Figures 2 through 15 represent only the *main* sources of facilitation. This was necessary for the sake of clarity. Although there were usually several factors involved, only the value function which *most* facilitated the enjoyment of another (or which *most* prevented it in the case of a negative value intensity) was indicated. The high degree of differentiation among patterns, therefore, may be seen as one result of limiting the use of facilitation to single factors.

7 • The Product of Separatism

The attitude constellation that we call Separatism is, of course, more than a vague corpus of shared beliefs, values, and goals. It is constantly being articulated and rearticulated as a very perceptible external product. From the revolt of the Patriotes through the FLQ and the Parti Québécois, Separatism has continually tended to create an external "product," a reality that could be perceived by the individual as corresponding to the interior reality of his most cherished hopes, dreams, and identity. This correspondence is essential to the individual's initially seeking a Separatist (that is, a pro-independence, rather than a federal) solution to his political, economic, social, and emotional needs. Ultimately, the correspondence between these "internal" and "external" realities is directly proportionate to the spread of Separatism, since individuals join the movement (or the Parti Québécois, as is usually the case today) when they perceive that their overall needs, as measured in terms of P, W, R, E, A, and HW are being met, and leave it when they think they are not.

The types and amounts of values in Proposition 1 relate in a very particular manner, then, to the perceived external product of the Separatist movement. The function (f) of Separatism must therefore be considered as both correspondence (c) with the values of an individual and satisfaction of his needs. More formally presented,

$$f = \begin{matrix} n\,P \\ n\,W \\ n\,R \\ n\,E \\ n\,A \\ n\,HW \end{matrix} \quad C$$

Chapter 4 was chiefly descriptive, in an attempt to show how a variety of individuals chose Separatism. The C factor is clearer in some interviews than in others, since certain respondents were more aware of the sources of their political beliefs. But in all cases, the persons interviewed had already incorporated much of the Separatist ideology, and as a general rule they referred to the perceived product only to take exception to it.[1] On an individual basis, therefore, the C factor is too elusive to be dealt with meaningfully.

But if we deal collectively with the responses of the sixteen French Canadians who believed in independence, and, instead, compare the results with the reality presented to them by the Parti Québécois and other contemporary writers, the results are much more satisfactory. The C factor assumes a current relevance, since what has been internalized in the past can now be taken as a given and compared with the current product of the Separatist movement, and its relevance to the analysis of the current functions of Separatism, is more precise. Here is a brief illustration.

Separatists, as whole, experienced more power as a result of their political choice. But so did federalists. Would a given individual, therefore, experience power in either case? Would a group of people? If they could be certain that other rewards and benefits would remain the same, why would they choose Separatism? It is here that the C factor becomes important. People chose Separatism because they believe that a certain type of power is important, and the Parti Québécois offered more of it. There is thus an essential correspondence between the nature of power offered by the Parti Québécois and the nature of power experienced by Separatists. The degree of correspondence may vary, but it is nevertheless essential to each of the six functions of Separatism.

In order to give some structure to the analysis here a very general definition will be given for each of the six functions of Separatism. It represents an attempt to delineate the six general functions so that their interrelations will be perceived. The specific nature of each function—the ways in which it was experienced on a daily basis—has already been expressed in the individual interviews. This will be discussed here in terms of both *mode* and *facilitation*. It should be emphasized, of course, that the structure of these interviews was based on the anticipated structure of this analysis: the persons interviewed were asked to discuss the specific functions of Separatism according to six major areas defined in the interview. Many were forced to think about Separatism in new ways and said so. But the questions were open-ended and each respondent was given ample opportunity to answer as he wished. At the end of each interview it was felt that both questions and answers had been mutually understood by the interviewer and the respondent. Any subsequent interpretation of the material gained in interviews will, of necessity, take this understanding into account. There is thus a twofold coherence to be recognized here. The first is the understanding between interviewer and respondent. The second is the correspondence between "interior" and "exterior" reality, which has already been described as the C factor.

NOTES

1. For example, Philippe Beauséjour was concerned about the effect of Separatism on Quebec's economy, which seemed incapable of renewing itself. This was a frequent criticism (I_{15}; I_{23}). Georges Caron insisted that sovereignty implied only a political option, not an economic one. Sebastian Dupré thought Separatism was capable of becoming repressive, although he saw no immediate danger.

8 • Power

Power has many faces. Opinion is divided over the bases on which it rests, the nature and degree of coercion required for its exercise, and the issue of whether or not it can exist in potential (or latent) form.[1] In its broadest expression, Power is "a certain kind of human relationship"[2]; more closely defined, it is "the chance of a man or of a number of men to realize their own will in a communal action even against the resistance of others who are participating in the action." Power in this instance is potential: one can hold power without actually having prevailed in a given conflict. It is only necessary that the potential, the "chance" be there.[3] Laswell and Kaplan define Power still more tightly: "Power is participation in the making of decisions." It involves both policy and policy process—"the formulation, promulgation and application of identifications, demands and expectations concerning the future interpersonal relations of the self."[4]

To choose among definitions of power, even on a purely theoretical basis, is not easy. To do so for the purpose of examining its function in a given society is harder still. The chosen definition of power will be reflected in the definition of other values in the structure, and will determine the way in which many of the functional relationships are described. The best guides to the selection of a definition are the specific requirements of this study.

To begin with, a functional analysis requires a structure that is flexible enough to incorporate all of the relevant data. Categories need not be mutually exclusive, but together they do have to be inclusive of all the material under analysis. A second requirement is an empirical correspondence with the ideas about power held by Separatists. This is similar to the understanding between interviewer and respondent described above, but it is more than that. It involves a reassessment of each category in terms of the experience uncovered. In the case of a movement such as Separatism, power is ephemeral, fleeting. Yet it would not do at all to discount the power that the individuals who were interviewed claimed to have got from

Separatism, or the other benefits that come to them through the power of the movement. Separatist power did not begin in November 1976, but with the growth of the movement.

The definition of power as "a relationship that offers the chance of realizing one's own will" appears to satisfy, in a broad sense at least, those two main requirements. To be sure, it frequently does involve "participation in the making of decisions," but not always. Political power in Quebec has always had its peculiarly passive elements, and membership in the Parti Québécois recalls in certain respects the blind faith with which French Canadians trusted their Church to act for them. The definition of power as the chance to realize one's own will takes this passivity into account, while it also incorporates the notion of personal power (which usually offers more intense and more immediate satisfaction) and avoids drawing an arbitrary line of demarcation between the two.

The elements of Power to be described here include, then, all those ways in which Separatism has brought to the individuals interviewed "the chance . . . to realize their own will in a communal action, even against the resistance of others who are participating in the action." The totality of these elements constitutes the power function of Separatism. A review of the ways in which Separatists interviewed experienced power yielded these results:

1. Sebastian Dupré (I_7) has gained significant moral authority because the values he has expressed publicly correspond in both substance and intensity with those in the community. Separatism also gives him a certain degree of intellectual freedom by providing an issue important enough to guarantee his right to be heard. The collective strength of the movement gives him some assurance that he will not be penalized too severely for expressing unorthodox views, and it also offers an intellectual setting in which he can realize his own identity. Finally, his election as a representative of parish pastors in the under-forty age group gives him a role in Church politics.

2. The two revolutionaries (I_{11}) have Power, but insist that they have no personal power. Because of their ideology, their contribution to the collective power of the movement is returned to them not as personal power but as identity.

3. Like the revolutionaries, Jacques Roche (I_{12}) has experienced Power not so much personally as collectively, chiefly as a member of his union and his nation. On a personal level, he experiences power chiefly in terms of more freedom.

4. Roger (I_{15}) experiences Power chiefly in the sense of having options, or choices, and being able to meaningfully withhold his vote. He no longer feels powerless to determine the direction of his own future.

5. Hélène, a waitress, has experienced little Power as yet, since she is not of voting age, but she anticipates greater recognition of her rights as a result of Separatism. For this reason, she will vote for the PQ when she is eligible.

6. Phillippe Beauséjour, a provincial bureaucrat, (I_{18}), has suffered a diminution of personal power due to conflict with the present power structure.

7. For Jean Dupont (I_{19}), a mechanic, being a member of a mass movement powerful enough to affect changes means that he no longer feels insignificant. The power of the PQ serves as a counterbalance against the despair and futility that has shadowed much of his adult life. On an individual level, the movement has brought him an increased awareness of his rights.

8. Claude Morin, formerly professor of Public Administration at the Université de Québec and subsequently Minister of Intergovernmental Affairs, gave up an important Provincial position when he left the Liberal party to join the PQ. He lost formal authority, but gained in terms of influence, due to Respect from both sides for his moral integrity. In 1972 he ran for the provincial legislature, but lost. Nevertheless, he thus had a chance to realize his own will against the resistance of the Liberals. Within the PQ he has ample opportunity to realize his own will, making decisions that range from choosing campaign slogans ("J'ai le goût de Québec") to platforms and strategy. His decision also made it possible to publish two books on federal-provincial relations that might otherwise have endangered his career.

9. Pierre Martin, a college student, says that membership in the PQ gives him potential Power. He, in turn, contributes to the strength of a movement that will ensure him of his rights.

10. Edgar Dion (I_{22}), a distinguished octogenarian, believes that individuals have more Power as a consequence of Separatism. He regards the PQ as only the most recent (and most successful) phase of a movement that has been developing for well over a century. He thinks that the movement has guaranteed the political and linguistic rights of individuals by serving as a "watchdog."

11. Martin Blain (I_{23}), a site inspector, feels that collective Power has not yet been realized, but he finds that the literature and information distributed by the party help maintain his personal influence within his union.

12. For Paul Martin (I_{25}), the father of Pierre, recognition of the rights of French Canadians by English-speaking Canadians has been the chief way in which he experiences Power.

13. Georges Caron (I_{27}) experiences Power as intellectual authority within the Separatist movement. His writings have been incorporated into the literature of the PQ and he lectures frequently throughout the province. In addition, he is a member of the city council of Ste.-Foy and has twice been a candidate for the provincial legislature.

14. There was insufficient information as to the Power experienced by the boys in the pool (as reflected in the neutral 3 designated on Table 1).

Power, for a developing political party or movement, is never the same as for a party or regime in office. For a number of reasons, the two can never be qualitatively compared. Michels discovered long ago that those who wield power are transformed themselves.[5] The fact that PQ was not actually *in* power was the single most important distinction between its power and that of the Liberal party, and it was also the fundamental difference between the Power experienced by Separatists and that experienced by federalists. For no matter how hard we try to limit the analysis of Power to its current functions, the problem of actual versus potential still influences the way in which people experience Power. Those who have a vested interest in change will experience Power differently from those whose main interest is in keeping the status quo. Similarly, the way in which they experience Power appears to affect their interest in maintaining or rejecting the status quo. Those who hold important decision-making positions in government and business tend to be staunch supporters of federalism, while those who have never had this type of power are more likely (than the successful) to believe in Separatism.[6] At the other end of the economic scale, those who tended to experience Power in terms of security were also inclined to support federalism, since for them maintenance of the status quo was essential.

Those who chose Separatism experienced Power quite differently. With the exception of the few activists who enjoyed decision-making power, most of the Separatists spoke long and passionately about the rights they now enjoyed—or would soon have—even without independence. These rights, they made it clear, were a direct result of Separatism, the first victory after a series of long and hard-fought battles; they also represented an increased chance for realizing the ultimate goal, independence. They represented the realization of their collective will and the chance to realize it even more fully in the future.

If these rights were facilitated by Respect, they were nevertheless experienced as Power. In 14 interviews, a total of 7 respondents stated that they or French Canadians in general had experienced Power as rights. But the nature of these rights were frequently unspecified, and was usually defined with difficulty, only after probing. Most of them were acutely aware of their position as members of an ethnic minority, yet they made little if any distinction between their rights within Canada generally and their rights within the province of Quebec. They blamed Ottawa for the failure of both the federal and provincial governments to guarantee them.

These rights were loosely defined in the interviews as economic equality and cultural autonomy. It was generally believed that two main factors contributed most to the achievement of these rights. These were an improved status of the French language,[7] and in Quebec a vastly improved and expanded educational program, designed to bring middle-calss status within the reach of anyone who aspired to it. These changes, however, were regarded as temporary solutions, attempts by the federal and provincial governments to stem the growing tide of dissatisfaction among French Canadians. Their high cost, in economic terms, only served to convince many of the Separatists that the governments involved—especially the federal—still profited enormously from keeping Quebec in the confederation, often at Quebec's expense. At the same time both governments acknowledged that Quebec's demands would be taken seriously, thus recognizing the Separatist movement as their competitor in the campaign for Quebec.

In comparing the Parti Québécois with "a watchdog," Edgar Dion echoed the sentiments of most of the Separatists interviewed. There was a broad consensus that only the threat of an independent Quebec had been sufficient to bring about policies designed for Quebec's benefit, most notably bilingualism. This view was shared by many of the French Canadian federalists; what distinguished them from their Separatist counterparts was the attitude that, having won such enormous concessions, Quebec could now benefit most by "putting up" *(se débrouiller)* with the rest of Canada, and that any continued militancy on the part of Separatists would be counterproductive. Yet, as Claude Morin, the political scientist who gave up a responsible position in the Liberal party to join the PQ maintains, the gains that have been attributed to Quebec in the areas of cultural autonomy, social and economic planning are minimal, and have been offset by the mighty central drift of power in Canada.[8] For this reason Morin and a good many *Péquistes* who were less articulate than he believed that independence was the only solution that could bring about full equality and ensure cultural survival. In the Separatist experience, the positive political and economic benefits that had thus far been achieved were of secondary importance when compared with these primary goals.

Practically speaking, the Separatist movement experienced its greatest increase in Power in terms of sheer size. In August 1973, the membership of the PQ was estimated to be 70,000, and a vigorous membership drive was under way. By October 29, when the provincial elections were held, the Parti Québecois polled 892,644 votes,[9] more than in the 1970 election and an increase from 23 to over 30 percent of the popular vote. When asked, "What is the main source of strength for the Parti Québécois?" Louis Bernard, then administrative assistant to Camille Laurin, the chief of the PQ's Parliamentary wing, replied, "The members." He discounted any of the party's functions, within or outside the legislature, as sources of Power, since the PQ, he said, was not interested in coalition with any of the other parties in the legislature. Unlike the conventional "cadre" party, the PQ would one day realize its true strength via a parliamentary majority. Until then, its most important task was educational, to convince more French Canadians of the merits and viability of the Parti Québécois.[10]

Nevertheless, there was in this burgeoning of the PQ's membership at least an element of Power, one that was felt and identified by the individuals who experienced it. When Jean Dupont said, "I have a kind of power, but if there's three million like me, that'll be power," he was expressing a new kind of identification, one that forced him to identify his own needs with those of other Separatists, and the needs of other Separatists with his own. This element of Power, which was experienced as identity, and strongly facilitated by Enlightenment, involved an intensification of relationships with one another and the recognition and articulation of a political will. As such, it was the first step toward a political victory.

If we look again at Figures 1–15, we can see that Power is repeatedly facilitated by two values, Respect and Enlightenment. Power, in turn, contributes so substantially to Enlightenment that the two values are mutually facilitative. This special relationship can best be explained in terms of the traditional linkage of Power and Enlightenment in Quebec society, when both values emanated from the authority of the Church. While they no longer proceed in identical ways from the Parti Québécois, there is a long-standing tendency to look for an external source of leadership and authority, especially in political affairs. Of the Separatists interviewed, five indicated that their political activities (party membership, voting, campaign activity) were the result of information received directly from the Parti Québécois. Five others were so committed to

Separatism after studying the information available to them, that they too might be classed as ideologues. In concentrating on an education campaign, the Parti Québécois appears to have been extremely successful in increasing both the domain and intensity of Separatism. In its campaign literature, especially the pamphlet *Quad nous serons vraiment chez nous,* and in its ambitious predictions prior to the 1973 election, the PQ did much more than present a platform and campaign for votes. It offered an image of power that, although it could hardly have been anticipated with any degree of reality, was convincing enough to be identified with Power itself. This image of power, presented as the only means of preserving "the French fact in North America," the identity and culture of the French Canadian nation, had broad appeal to those who considered themselves first Quebecers and only secondarily Canadians. Its appeal was based also on the fact that it held out a possibility, at least, of redressing the constitutional grievances which had been at issue for nearly two decades.[11] Its relationship with the elected provincial government was happily ambiguous, for it could claim credit for those reforms which resembled its own proposals, while arguing at the same time that (without independence) the changes would ultimately be meaningless.[12]

The question remains of course whether the majority of Quebec's citizens will develop a sufficient commitment to their national identity that they will be able to accept the PQ's most essential appeal, the doctrine that Quebec's nationalism can survive only within a sovereign state.

NOTES

1. For a discussion of this point, see Arnold Rose, *The Power Structure* (New York: Oxford University Press, 1967), pp. 45–48.

2. Carl J. Friedrich, *Constitutional Government and Politics* (New York: Harper Bros., 1937), p. 11, as quoted in Lasswell and Kaplan, *Power and Society,* p. 75.

3. Hans Gerth and C. Wright Mills (eds.), *From Max Weber: Essays in Sociology* (New York: Oxford University Press, 1946), p. 180.

4. Lasswell and Kaplan, *Power and Society,* p. 75.

5. Robert Michels, *Political Parties: A Sociological Study of the Oligarchical Tendencies of Modern Democracy* (New York: Collier Books, 1962).

6. This view is based on two interviews, one with the scholar mentioned above, who asked that he not be further identified, and one with Professor Maxwell Cohen, Dean of the Law School at McGill University.

7. The crucial position of the French language in securing these rights has been recog-

nized in the Gendron Report and by Gilbert Paquette and Raymond Lemieux in a pamphlet prepared by the Parti Québecois, *À Quand la reforme scolaire?* (Montreal, 1972).

8. Claude Morin, *Le Pouvoir Québécois en négotiation* (Montreal: Les Editions Boréal Express, 1972).

9. A total of 2,964,605 votes were cast. *Le Devoir*, November 3, 1973.

10. Interview, Quebec City, August 29, 1973.

11. See Daniel Johnson, Speech in the Quebec Legislature, April 23, 1963, in *Quebec States her Case*, Edited by Frank Scott and Michael Oliver (Toronto: Macmillan of Canada, 1968), pp. 31–40. Johnson, then leader of the opposition party, the *Union Nationale* argued that federalism had approximately three more years to prove its effectiveness in dealing with the issues. While this rhetoric was essentially a challenge to the Liberal Party to prove that their particular brand of federalism could work in the three years remaining before the next election, it also outlined the very real difficulties inherent in the present structure.

12. Claude Morin, *op. cit.*; Claude Morin, *Le Combat Québecois* (Montreal: Les Editions du Boréal Express, 1973), pp. 177–83.

9 • Wealth

Economically, Separatism brought no discernible benefit to the individuals interviewed. Most of them, in fact, anticipated no immediate economic benefits even with independence. As a group, the Separatists interviewed were less concerned about Wealth than any other benefit that independence might provide. They displayed, on the average, a sophisticated understanding of the relationship between personal and national wealth, but were willing to sacrifice for the latter, which they considered more important.

It is possible to speak of political, economic, and social functions of Wealth: the political function of wealth is to preserve the stability and independence of the state in pursuing its determined goals; its economic function is to aid the flow of production and trade, and its social function to create a classless or class society, depending on its pattern of distribution. The anticipated benefits of Wealth as a function of Separatism followed this structure. Most of the Separatists interviewed felt that the most important economic function of the Separatist movement would be the political function, the securing of sufficient credit, resources and means of production to allow Quebec to achieve and maintain independence without in turn becoming dependent on the United States or some other external power. The economic function of Wealth was considered important only to the extent that an improved flow of production and trade could aid the political goal. As an end in itself, wealth was relatively unimportant for the Separatists. This was reflected by its comparatively low intensity (3.07). As a social factor, however, Wealth was considerably more important. At least five of the Separatists interviewed spoke favorably of the social consequences a redistribution of wealth would bring. This redistribution, involving the creation of thousands of new jobs and a minimum wage of $2.50 per hour, was a widely publicized plank in the PQ's program. Its aim was to bring an element of dignity to the lives of French Canadians by ending their economic "enslavement"; however, this could be fully accomplished only through political independence.[1]

On an individual basis, the expectation of future Wealth played a far more significant role than its present enjoyment. The promise of Separatism has given large numbers of workers the prospect of joining the middle class. Hélène, the seventeen-year-old waitress, expected to gain more desirable employment and a higher standard of living in a few years. She planned to vote for the Parti Québécois when she became eighteen, because, in her own words, "I don't want to be turned over to the manual-labor force." Sebastian Dupré, whose own economic status dropped considerably as a result of his espousal of Separatism, anticipates profound changes in the economic status of his parishioners, once the sources of inequality are removed. Jean and Robert, members of the internationalist Socialist Workers' League (Ligue Socialiste Ouvrière) look forward to the creation of a classless society, even though they have suffered severe economic setbacks—in terms of being excluded from the job market—because of their political activities. Pierre, the eighteen-year-old student and son of Paul Martin, the businessman, is still quite insulated from the economic consequences of politics, but he is sufficiently committed to a redistribution of wealth to have joined the Parti Québécois, which, he believes, will create a more equitable and consequently a more viable social system. In general, the relative economic deprivations incurred as a result of Separatism were more than compensated for by high hopes for the future. To those who had gained nothing in current terms, Separatism held out not only other forms of compensation but the promise that there would be sufficient Wealth to accomplish the desired political and social goals.

Still others had already experienced positive benefits. Within certain areas of employment, most notably the arts and education, being Separatist often makes it easier to get jobs. Jacques Roche, for example, found his university job in this way. In his opinion, the respect and affection of one's colleagues is based not only on a community of interests, but on a concrete sociological fact: those who have accepted Separatism are more aware, more stable individuals who, in accepting Separatism, have come to terms with themselves and their problems of national and social identity. They have thus attained a stage of personal development that those who espouse federalism have not yet achieved, and may therefore be regarded as more competent. In certain fields of employment, then, Separatism carries a presumption of competence that results in a distinct economic advantage for the individual.

To others, chiefly those in the lower wage brackets, Separatism brought some measure of success, through an increased confidence in their capabilities and ability to succeed. Jean Dupont, for example, had been helped toward an understanding of his own economic predicament in a way that was most beneficial. Once he was able to isolate the external causes of his repeated failures (a poor education, lack of self-esteem as a result of Anglo-Canadian attitudes), he gained sufficient self-respect so that he was able to open a small shop. Whereas he had held no previous job for more than two years, his gas station and repair shop were netting him one hundred dollars per week, and, although he estimated that taxes took nearly 45 percent of this small income, he was pleased with his own success and generally optimistic about the future.

A few had benefited substantially. Georges Caron's success was due in large measure to his open espousal of Separatism and the respect he enjoyed as a result of his professed commitment. His successes, both with his *Journal de Ste.-Foy* and his restaurants in downtown Quebec, stood out as two examples of the profits to be made in Quebec. Independence, he said, offered the most viable economic future for Quebec, and he had had sufficient confidence in that future to invest in it early. If he had had the good fortune to realize profits under the existing federal structure, he did not complain. The main source of his success had been his faith in the future of Quebec, and this faith had been enormously profitable to him.

There was also a very indirect way in which many individuals, including federalists, profited from Separatism. French Canadians are getting better jobs now, and the middle class is expanding. This change has been implemented not only by the increased affluence of the last twenty years, but by the new respect in which French Canadians are held.

Wealth does not appear to be a significant value among those French Canadians who have chosen Separatism. In two cases, Wealth conflicts with a preferred value, such as Enlightenment (I_7) or Power (I_{18}), but in four more instances it has no significance, being merely compatible with these values, such as Englightenment (I_{17}, I_{23}) and Power I_{20}, I_{21}). While there are no perceptible gains here, the individual's value position in these four instances is satisfactory because of the supporting role played by Enlightenment or Power. Thus, Hélène, the waitress, experienced neither a gain nor a loss in terms of Wealth, but she was satisfied with the situation because her *understanding* of it indicated that significant gains could be had only at some future date. Again, Martin Blain was satisfied with his economic status because he understood that the Parti Québécois could do nothing to improve it until it won a parliamentary victory. For Claude Morin, the politician and university professor, the loss in income was more than compensated for by an increase in Power, while for Pierre Martin, the student, an increase in Wealth was of secondary importance when compared with an increase in Power. Wealth, it appears, is easily compensated for by other values. Whether an individual experiences a loss or fails either to lose or gain, the conflicting or compensating values remain the same. For those who did experience a gain, the pattern is slightly different. As might be expected, three people gained perceptibly, and these gains were facilitated by Power. One person's (I_{27}) gain was facilitated by Enlightenment (although in his case, self-respect played a significant role), and two others may be considered to have experienced increased Wealth because of Respect, one directly (I_{12}) and the other indirectly (I_{22}).

As an immediate individual benefit, Wealth was of virtually no significance in the decision to support Separatism. As a future benefit, Wealth did have some significance, both individually and on a national scale. Of the Separatists interviewed, six saw compelling economic reasons for independence, and said so spontaneously. All of these individuals except Hélène, the waitress, expected these gains to be national as well as personal, with a "repatriation" of Quebec's wealth serving a function that was both political and social.

The correspondence between the individual's needs and the perceived product of the PQ is easily seen. However, in this case it is a correspondence of hope—of the individual's present frustration and hope for a better life in the future with the promise of the PQ. Since most of us are compelled to live in an economic world, we experience Wealth or lack of it in innumerable daily transactions. But our understanding of Wealth is limited by the vastness and complexity of the economic system. The role of the PQ is expanding the individual's comprehension of Wealth is thus more significant than in any other category. Those who feel victimized by an economic system they fail to comprehend are most receptive to an ideology that not only offers a solution but promises that this time they will be masters of their own fate.

The economic arguments for independence varied, as did the attitudes supporting the other values. Yet there was a great deal more coherence among these arguments for Separatism than among those geared toward any other value. As Table 1 indicates, there less was gained, currently, in terms of Wealth than any other value. However, most of the respondents who were Separatists believed that they would ultimately benefit, and quite significantly. Independence would be to their immense advantage, since union was costly—and hope was cheap.

NOTES

1. This type of "enslavement" is a recurrent theme. Sebastian Dupré has devoted his life to freeing people from it, and Jean Dupont expressed similar feelings with regard to the heavy tax burden he is forced to shoulder.

10 • Respect

The value Respect may be divided into two elements, respect from others and self-respect. Lasswell and Kaplan's eight categories include rectitude and righteousness, while Lane uses "moral needs and values" and "esteem needs and values."[1] In the interview situation, it was found that the term *Respect* was easily and broadly understood since it was capable of being related to a broader range of experience than any other value. Respect, or lack of it, appears to be the most emotionally significant of all values, at least among French Canadians. The way in which it is experienced, however, marks an important difference between federalists and Separatists. Most federalists spoke of mutual respect among ethnic groups, chiefly the Anglo-Canadians and French Canadians. Some of them felt that Separatists had specifically excluded themselves from this "community of respect" by their outrageous demands, and that this threatened all French Canadians. They viewed mutual Respect not only as the cornerstone of confederation, but as the chief guarantor of their rights within it. They were thus quick to condemn any movement that threatened it. Yet even while emphasizing the mutual quality of this Respect, at least one respondent indicated that this mutuality was based on the good will of Anglo-Canadians. "The President of Air Canada, for example, is a reasonable man," stated one high-level federalist bureaucrat (I_2), "but what would he think of us if Quebec were to go independent? What would his options be?" This kind of "mutual" respect appears to be an admixture of benevolence and fear.

Federalists also thought much less spontaneously about self-respect than did Separatists. Even where the term *self-respect* was fully understood,[2] the federalists tended to use more external criteria than did the Separatists. The terms *self-esteem* and *integrity* were heard frequently. There was relatively little emphasis on identity; their theoretical position did not demand it, and there was no emphasis on an expanding awareness of self. Self-respect for federalists was considerably less important than other modes of

Respect. In those cases (I_4, I_5, I_8, I_{16}, I_{24}) where it was based on a particular identity, the identification was always with a class or an elite.

By contrast, the Separatists interviewed spoke more volubly about self-respect than about any other form of respect. Here, self-respect was much more broadly understood and discussed, frequently incorporating aspects of Enlightenment and Affection. For Philippe Beauséjour (I_{18}), it will be remembered, self-respect was a logical and factual prerequisite to the respect of others. Jacques Roche and Jean Dupont expressed similar ideas. For perhaps half of the Separatists, there was a discernible attitude that Separatism had made possible in a way that prior nationalist movements had never done a positive and pleasant identification as a French Canadian which did more to raise their self-esteem than anything else. This identification was non-elitist and classless; it was a cultural and linguistic identification. Since the movement demanded that commitment to it rule out all question of compromise with any other identification (such as with class or with Canada) the nagging questions of inferiority that had plagued French Canadians for well over a century were obviated. Several persons spoke of the pride that they were able to feel. At least three of the respondents described spontaneously the feelings of shame they had about being French Canadian prior to joining the Separatist movement.

In the course of these interviews, it became apparent that Separatism had given its adherents the ability—that it had authorized them—to feel certain emotions that had hitherto been prohibited. As Martin Blain, the site inspector, said, "It has validated our values." For certain people, Separatism appears to have replaced religious tradition as the dominant ideology. It offers a preconceived identity and certain standards of experience (pride, righteousness) and behavior (activism, inquiry) that give structure and meaning to their lives.

Aside from the possible political Power it might bring, the Separatists claimed to care little about the Respect of others outside the movement. Many of them felt that their goals in this regard had been achieved, but that without a commensurate increase in power these gains would in time be eroded. Those who gained Respect tended to get it from their peers, chiefly in terms of admiration and moral influence.

While a majority of the federalists interviewed tended to achieve Respect as a result of Power, nearly all of the Separatists experienced Respect as a result of Enlightenment.[3] This difference in facilitation is almost as striking as the difference in mode. A significant number of federalists (five) did experience Respect as a result of Enlightenment. With the exception of one person, these individuals had earned respect through their carefully considered positions regarding the issue of independence for Quebec. Separatism thus played a significant role in bringing Respect to a cross section of individuals, both Separatist and federalist, and in the case of both groups this Respect has been facilitated to some degree by the rethinking and reassessment of the relative merits of retaining or rejecting the notion of a pluralist, bi-ethnic society. What is significant here, though, is that for approximately two-thirds of the Separatists interviewed, Respect was facilitated by Enlightenment, while for over half of the federalists, it was facilitated by Power. It is difficult to isolate cause and effect here, but it would appear that those French Canadians who chose Separatism tended to be motivated less by a drive for Power than those who did not. They derived satisfaction more from an increased self-respect than from the respect of others, and the recognition and acceptance of their present state of powerlessness did nothing to decrease it. There was, of course, another face to this "powerless" pose: in recognizing the present condition, they could lay the basis for a more powerful future. But the fact remains that in Quebec only Separatists appeared capable of maintaining self-respect while admitting and accepting powerlessness. This loose linkage, this ability to leave security behind, in order to reach for a better future, appears to be a psychological tendency unique among the Separatists.

If we consider the traditional role of Enlightenment in Quebec culture, this is not surprising. The function of Enlightenment in facilitating Respect and consequentially self-respect dates back to the period after conquest, when both Power and Enlightenment reposed in the Church. If the clergy was hardly in a position to confer the former, it could surely dispense the latter, although one had to be worthy of it.[4] With political power unattainable, Enlightenment became the traditional measure of respect. Those who now turn for reassurance and a sense of security to the "truth" embodied in Separatism are in fact repeating a very old social pattern. There is thus a profound correspondence between the sociology of respect in the old order and that which exists in the new. For those who (whether for lack of opportunity or lack of grace) were never assimilated into a Canadian identity, Separatism continues the Church's role.

There is, of course, a difference. The identity that the Church conferred was one that brought to the individual a dignity that transcended the meanness of everyday life. It reached out toward Rome and spiritual communion with the Catholic world; at the same time it reached backwards in history, past the secular era, past the Reformation, to the models of the Christian martyrs. The identity that Separatism offers is, by contrast, steeped in time and place. The dignity that it offers is based not on trancendence but upon recognition and resolve. The self-reliance that is so essential to Separatist politics is a declaration of independence not only from "Anglo-Saxon" domination, but from dependence on the Church as well, and is thus a new and different source of Respect.

The Respect that French Canadians experience as a result of Separatism corresponds more directly than any other value with their perceived needs. and is thus the most compelling reason for supporting the movement. It was widely expressed that *all* French Canadians had benefited in this way, and that those who remained federalist had helped themselves to undeserved rewards while doing little or nothing to support or strengthen the movement which had brought them these benefits. Even Jeanne Nadeau admitted this. But the former president of the Liberal party in Quebec accused Separatists of "taking advantage" of the gains won by the hard work of the Liberal party.[5] There was thus a tendency to credit these advances to either side, depending on the degree and direction of one's commitment; however, moderates on both sides were willing to give credit to the other where they felt it was due.

Separatism answers the needs of French Canadians for Respect because it reaffirms a collective past and its cultural and social consequences in a way that no bi-ethnic or bi-cultural approach can afford to. It asserts the primacy of French Canadian culture, and in so doing recognizes it as a goal too valid to be compromised by inept and inappropriate political arrangements.

NOTES

1. Robert E. Lane, *Political Thinking and Consciousness* (Chicago: Markham Publishing Co., 1968), pp. 37–41.

2. The French equivalent, *amour propre*, has a slightly different meaning, which is difficult to convey in English. Therefore the French version of the questionnaire phrased the question, "Do you respect yourself more, as a result of being Separatist (federalist)?" Some respondents went on to discuss *amour propre;* some did not.

3. In nine out of fourteen cases Respect was facilitated by Enlightenment. However, one of these was a negative facilitation. Hélène, the waitress, suffered a decrease in respect from her peers, who were mainly working-class adolescents, as a result of her knowledge.

4. Here it might be worthwhile to contemplate the Latin word for worthy, *dignus*. In French as well as English, the word *dignity* is derived from it. Despite the difference in syntax, those schooled in Latin cannot help but associate the two.

5. Interview with Claude Frenette, Montreal, June 29, 1973.

11 • Enlightenment

Any attempt to assess the effects of Separatism on the operations of the intellect must of necessity be limited in scope. The term *Enlightenment* encompasses a variety of elements, from ideology through ideas, understanding and explanation to knowledge, understanding, and skills. These elements may be grouped together because they can be related to (or distinguished from) the other value symbols in a relatively similar manner. In the interviews, an attempt was made to encourage spontaneous discussion of all forms of Enlightenment, but the limitations of the situation made it necessary to direct the conversation toward four main points, consciousness of history, culture, and class, general information, formal education, and ideology. The last question (15.0) was asked in connection with some general questions about Separatist versus federalist attitudes, and did not usually receive so intense concentration as the more personal questions (6.0 through 12.2).

An interesting result was that most Separatists did not believe there was a Separatist ideology. There was a general consensus that the movement consisted of a series of spontaneous responses to a crisis situation. However they credited the Parti Québécois with having defined the situation and having alerted them to it, thus describing the PQ's most significant function in keeping itself in power.

If the PQ is now the main source of information, it draws its material from a vast array of sources. For example, the main points of the argument for independence were expressed in 1961, seven years before the PQ was formed, by Marcel Chaput in *Why I Am a Separatist*. Essentially, Chaput argued that the French Canadian nation, like all other nations, required autonomy in order to function. Without autonomy, it could not survive, and autonomy was impossible without political independence.[1] This reasoning was utilized, in 1965, in the waning years of the Union Nationale, by Daniel Johnson, in *Egalité ou Indépendance*.[2] There are, in addition, contemporary sources. Claude Ryan was not a Separatist and in 1977 became the leader of Quebec's Liberals, but his editorials were read almost routinely by the more intellectual members of the movement. Other writers and scholars, such as Claude Morin and Marcel Rioux, the sociologist, have independently taken positions supporting Separatism, and their ideas are widely discussed.

Whether or not there is a Separatist ideology, then, is largely a matter of definition. Maxwell Cohen, dean of the Law School at McGill University, believes there is an ideology because

> . . . what matters is there is that degree of group feeling which causes a certain degree of mobilization leading to certain apparently commonly believed-in goals by the group, and once you're able to abstract that from the body of human experience across time and space, you're able to say, "I've got an ideology" about it. I think you can fairly say that to the extent that *any* ideology exists in the field of nationalism . . . there is some of it in the mystique of French Canadian nationalist-separatist sentiment.[3]

The most prevalent definition of ideology is the one inherited from Marx, as reinterpreted by Mannheim, who, while accepting Marx's view of it as a self-perpetuating cultural superstructure, both universalized it (to include even Marxism), and refined it, distinguishing "ideologies," which perpetuate ongoing systems, from "utopias," which, if successful, cause the breakup of an established system and the creation of a new order.[4] The special problems of dealing with a developing situation such as Separatism make this distinction unworkable here, for, as Willard A. Mullins notes, "a crucial problem with the distinction is that one cannot tell when thought is utopian except in the successful case where norms serve to shatter the present order, and only after they do. Analysis must always be *post facto*."[5] To apply this distinction to Separatism would be to characterize it as at once ideological and utopian: ideological for those who believed in it; utopian for those who were as yet uncommitted.

Lasswell and Kaplan offer the notion of the "political myth," which, because of its compatability with the value index used here and its emphasis on the function of these symbols, will be used here. The political myth is the "pattern of basic political symbols current in a society." The "pattern of basic political symbols," revealed by data gathered in the interviews with Separatists was composed of (1) a specific Separatist value pattern, (2) a type of historical consciousness, and (3) general information.

The specific Separatist value pattern (1) may be assessed in two ways. The first is by analyzing the relative frequency with which Separatism supports the six symbolic values. Those values which contribute most frequently to the enjoyment of the others may be said to have a *high* frequency, and may be considered significant values within a given society. Those which contribue least frequently may be said to have a *low* frequency. Thus, within the Separatist value pattern Power and Enlightenment have the highest frequency (24 and 18 respectively); Respect has a frequency of 12, and Affection and Wealth show frequencies of 3 and 1, respectively.[6]

But what of the specific values which support Separatism? A second aspect of the Separatist value pattern is the attitudes intrinsic to belief in Separatism itself. Briefly summarized, these are as follows: (1) that French Canadians constitute a nation whose survival must be assured; (2) that this is impossible within the present constitutional structure; (3) that unless immediate action is taken, the French Canadian nation will be lost forever, though assimilation, migration, and the centripetal tendency of political power in Canada. The values Power, Enlightenment, and Respect each has a role in supporting these attitudes. Without Power, national survival *(la survivance nationale)*—and along with it, the preservation of one's intergal identity as French Canadian—is lost. Without Enlightenment, French Canadians will not know what they have lost until it is too late; in addition, they will continue to be cheated in their day-to-day transactions with the rest of Canada. Finally, Respect underlies the entire structure. If one has self-respect, he will be able to identify and insist on the other values. Only those who lack self-respect will not care about Power, or about the truth that can free them from bondage.

Here the notion of historical consciousness becomes important. In changing the consciousness of history, Separatism has had a significant impact in terms of Enlightenment, Respect, and Affection. Paradoxical though it may seem, it is in opening the possibility of independence that Separatism has been able to restructure Canadian history. Martin Blain, the site inspector, was aware of this when he said, "They have got to the bottom of the thing." Once independence is admitted as a possible and even viable solution, all of Quebec's history and the whole range of emotions about it become admissible as well. Conversely, any solution that stops short of independence must now pass over much of the feeling that has been evoked. For this reason alone, the Separatist movement is distinctly different from the nationalism of the 1930s.

One of the most important functions of Separatism was to structure and direct the general information available to the individual. Some, such as Roger, the salesman, and Edgar Dion, the retired chemist, thought that this had been the result of competition between the two factions. This view was echoed by the boys in the swimming pool when they replied that Separatism was good because they could no longer be lied to. Separatism also appeared to create a new atmosphere of curiosity, chiefly about public issues, although there was a general reluctance to interpret these matters individually. It seemed that there was still a distinction to be made between "sacred" and "profane" literature, between that which was essential and the merely frivolous. Only the subject had shifted, from man's heavenly to earthly destiny. As in the past, interpretation of important knowledge was left to an authority, in this case the Parti Québécois.

To the question, "Does Separatism function as an ideology?," the answer is yes. Despite the openness of Separatism as an intellectual system, and the variety of its sources, it may be said to function as an ideology because of the role it plays in the lives of its adherents. This function may be seen most clearly in the case of Sebastian Dupré, but it can be observed also in those of more sophisticated individuals such as Philippe Beauséjour, the bureaucrat, and Pierre Martin, the student.

Some French Canadians felt that formal educational opportunities had improved, as a result of Separatism, and that the reforms of the school system[7] had been undertaken in an effort to stem the growing tide of dissatisfaction with the offerings of federal and provincial governments. But they were cynical about the value of this "opportunity." Jean Dupont sneered that the CEGEP's were half empty, and that the new educational system was little more than a building program; Jacques Roche's assessment that "you cannot offer individual solutions [in terms of educational opportunities] to a problem which is collective" may more accurately reflect the situation.

The intense interaction of the two values Enlightenment and Respect is characteristic of an ideological system, and is perhaps essential to the development of a movement such as Separatism. For what other rewards are there to attract a mass following? Most of the Separatists interviewed believed that Power would not be fully realized for some time. Separatism had certainly not contributed to their economic success. Only in another area of great emotional significance, then, could Separatism offer a sufficiently compelling reward. The role that Respect—and its denial—has played in French Canadian history gives it this crucial importance, but as has been indicated, this importance is structured by the Separatist ideology.

If Respect is thus facilitated by Enlightenment, the converse is also true. From the interviews it became clear that Respect and self-respect provided an emotional atmosphere that made it possible to risk taking new and radical directions in thinking. Despite the ideological character of the movement, Separatists demonstrated a surprising open-mindedness and tolerance of ambiguity. Fourteen interviews revealed almost as many opinions as to the ideal form of government and relations with the rest of Canada. Throughout these interviews ran a unifying theme, the belief that since French Canadians were fully capable of running their own state, they should be given the opportunity to do so. Respect, in this case, was thus accompanied by a very specific imperative.

Because of the ways in which an ideology operates, there is a high correspondence between the type of enlightenment offered by Separatism and the type needed and desired by individuals. In changing and defining French Canadian history, for example, the Separatist movement has uncovered historical "facts" that have great emotional appeal, not only because they explain the past in a more acceptable way, but because they appear to have been suppressed by Federalist historians. The remark that French Canadians had been "lied to," made by the twelve-year-old boy in the pool, should be noted here again. As an ideology, Separatism constantly structures the information generally available, defining and redefining values in the process. It thus tends to bring the values of the individual into conformity with its own tenets.

NOTES

1. Marcel Chaput, *Why I Am a Separatist*, transl. by Robert A. Taylor (Toronto: Ryerson Press, 1961). Dr. Chaput was president of the R.I.N. *(Rassemblement pour l'Indépendance Nationale)*, which later merged with the *Mouvement Souveraineté-Association* and other parties to form the *Parti Québecois*.

2. Johnson, however, did not categorically rule out federalism as a means for guaranteeing national survival. He thus stopped short of his compatriots who insisted on independence.

3. Interview, Montreal, July 4, 1973.

4. Karl Mannheim, *Ideology and Utopia*, transl. by Louis Wirth and Edward Shils (New York: Harcourt, Brace and World, 1936 edition, n.d.).

5. "On the Concept of Ideology in Political Science," *American Political Science Review* 65 (June 1972): 498–510.

6. Contrast this with the intensities indicated in Table 1. Because of its dynamic nature, the facilitation patterns give a better indication of the *role* each value plays in supporting Separatism, *Cf.* supra, p. 000.

7. These were begun by the Liberals in 1964, following the recommendations of the Parent Commission. They thus antedated the rise of Separatism as a serious challenge to either major party. Whether or not the continuation of this program is a response to Separatism is problemmatical.

12 • Affection

Although Separatists gained quite perceptibly in terms of Affection, nearly all of them had difficulty in expressing precisely how they had benefited. In contrast with the high importance accorded to Respect, they appeared to consider Affection relatively unimportant, and had little to say about it. From the difficulty most respondents had in even superficial discussion of this function, it appeared that this value had traditionally been suppressed in French-Canadian culture. Several individuals chose to discuss affection in terms of loyalty;[1] three of them, without any prompting in that direction, said that they had experienced affection, but then went on to describe it as Respect. Paul Martin, for example, was suspicious of the increased friendliness of his (English-speaking) boss, but then interpreted it as a gesture of respect. For at least five people, Affection was experienced as, or through, a redefinition of values. Georges Caron said that by becoming more conscious of what his values were, he had been drawn closer to his family. Four others felt that this definition of values had made it easier to share common ideals and goals, and that this commonality made it easier to accept one another. The feeling of no longer being alone, expressed so poignantly by Sebastian Dupré, is one result of this new commonality.

Only two people, both highly educated and more articulate than the others, were able to express this newfound affection as freedom to enjoy one another. For Jacques Roche, the sociologist, it was the result of the "collective dimension" that Separatism had added to individual relationships; for Philippe Beauséjour, the bureaucrat, it was the "pleasure in discovering ourselves, the pleasure in discovering each other."

Affection was facilitated predominantly by Enlightenment, a finding that was anticipated, in view of the importance accorded to that value in French Canadian culture. The tendency to intellectualize, to withdraw from one's own feelings was a characteristic noted throughout interviews with both federalists and Separatists. As an ideology, Separatism continues this traditional linkage between Enlightenment and Affection, while at the same time defining and deepening the latter. It appears to be subtly altering the balance between the two.

It is difficult to assess the extent to which Separatism answers the needs of the individual for Affection. The limitations of the interview situation made it impossible to program the necessary questions in the questionnaire, and the respondents were unable or unwilling to speak spontaneously about this function, as they had on the preceding four. The need of all individuals for Affection and for objects of affection is widely recognized. What is not known is the degree to which French Canadians are aware of their need for Affection, or the position that Affection enjoys in comparison (or in competition) with the other values.

The Parti Québécois, among others, has attempted to define Quebec as an object of affection. One manifestation of this was the massive campaign, originally conceived as a prelude to the provincial election anticipated for 1974 (but called in October 1973 by the Liberal government), which bombarded the public with bumper stickers and billboards proclaiming, "J'ai le goût de Québec." The PQ has carefully avoided defining a "hate object," preferring instead to address its disapproval toward certain specific issues, chiefly economic, and it has also avoided the "racial" arguments prevalent in the 1930s, preferring to supplant these with the political issues of language and culture. It is this love of Quebec, as differentiated from love of each other, which corresponds most directly with the affections of the Separatists interviewed. Solange Chaput-Rolland, the journalist and author, speaks rapturously of "*ma terre-Québec* (my land, Quebec)"[2]; Georges Caron explained this feeling when he spoke of identifying, beneath his feet, a land where his parents and grandparents lived and died. This love for and identification with their land may be explained by the estrangement from France, the ambiguities of their relations with the rest of Canada, and above all the long and intimate relationship with forests and fields, first as *coureurs des bois* and later as tillers of the soil. In its manifest external product, then, the Parti Québecois corresponds only partially, but profoundly nevertheless, with the long-standing values of French Canadians.

NOTES

1. Question 11.0 was phrased, "Have you experienced any greater loyalty or affection from anyone as a result of the existence of Separatism?"

2. Solange Chaput-Rolland, *My Country, Canada or Quebec?* (Toronto: Macmillan of Canada, 1966).

13 • Health and Well-being

How does Separatism function in securing the physical and mental well-being of French Canadians? As the term implies, Health and Well-being encompass both physical and mental well-being. Unlike the first five functions, it is a composite, reflecting the specific value patterns of a given society. It may also be described as an equilibrium, a process that sustains itself through the use of symbolic values. The processes that combine to support a sense of well-being are admittedly more varied than those essential to health; however, mental and physical health are generally considered to be mutually supportive, and thus all of the functions come into play here, if not directly, then indirectly. The patterns of facilitation are therefore intrinsic to the understanding of this sixth and last function.

Sullivan's concept of the "self as system" can best be used to explain this complex function. Each individual, in the course of maturation, develops a dynamic process whose function is to avoid anxiety and preserve a sense of security: "The self-system, from its beginnings and throughout its historic development, tends always to resist significant change in the direction of living."[1] This process sustains itself through the use of symbols. The particular assortment—or configuration—of symbolic values needed to maintain this equilibrium varies from one culture and even from one individual to the next.

Sullivan goes so far as to say that, in most societies, Well-being is based on Power, specifically a sense of power in interpersonal relationships. The facilitation patterns would only partially support Sullivan's conclusion, although the field of analysis here is somewhat broader.[2] A review of the specific ways in which the individual respondents experienced Well-being as a result of their political commitment yields similar results:

1. Sebastian Dupré (I_7) has gained significantly in terms of a sense of companionship and emotional support through the affection of young parishioners.

2. The two revolutionaries (I_{11}) deny having any personal power, but their lives and a good deal of their interpersonal relations) are characterized by the power that they exercise in the name of the movement. Well-being is therefore experienced in terms of power and security in interpersonal relations.

3. Jacques Roche (I_{12}) experiences Well-being in terms of a sense of relatedness (which he refers to as "the collective dimension").

4. Roger (I_{15}) experiences Well-being in terms of personal control of the circumstances which shape his life.

5. Hélène, the waitress (I_{17}), gains Well-being in terms of hope, through an increased sense of power.

6. Philippe Beauséjour (I_{18}) experiences Well-being in terms of resolution of old anxiety-provoking conflicts through enlightenment.

7. Jean Dupont (I_{19}) experiences Well-being as emotional support (through Enlightenment) and hope (through an increased sense of collective Power).

8. Like Philippe Beauséjour, Claude Morin (I_{20}) appears to gain Well-being in terms of resolving old anxiety-provoking conflicts through Enlightenment. If he has lost Power on the national scene, he has nevertheless gained on the Provincial level (despite the loss of his formal authority). It would appear that he has gained Power in those relationships which are significant to him.

9. Pierre Martin (I_{21}) experiences Well-being in terms of a sense of commitment (as opposed to alienation) because the Power of the PQ, to which he belongs, provides an opportunity for meaningful participation.

10. Edgar Dion (I_{22}) experiences the satisfaction that his long-founded hopes are being recognized through the Power of the PQ.

11. Martin Blain (I_{23}) experiences Well-being in terms of resolution of old anxiety-provoking doubts about his values.

12. For Paul Martin (I_{25}), Separatism has brought relief from the pressures of cultural conflict, and self-acceptance, through increased Respect from others.

13. Georges Caron (I_{27}) experiences Well-being in terms of control over his own life through increased personal and political Power.

14. The boys in the pool (I_{28}) appear to enjoy Well-being as hope for their future. From the remark, "They will no longer be able to lie to us," and the confidence expressed therein, it would appear that their optimism is based on the Respect they experience.

Whether possessing power as an ethnic minority can be compared with possessing power in interpersonal relations is a point worth considering. It was a personal impression that the experience of despair, powerlessness, and futility on the national level was not only symbolic of, but reflected in, countless daily transactions. For example, the humiliation that Jean Dupont experienced as the result of his social and economic milieu was reflected in his relations with people he met. He found it difficult to become intimate with others because of his need, even in the United States, to deny being French Canadian.

What is most significant is that in half the cases Power did not directly facilitate Well-being. It would appear that, in French Canada at least, certain other values contribute to the sense of Well-being, and it is not surprising that the chief one should be Enlightenment. But in every case, one or the other of these two values was either the primary or the secondary facilitator of Health and Well-being. Enlightenment was the primary facilitator in three cases and the secondary facilitator in seven others, while Power was a primary facilitator in seven cases and a secondary facilitator in three others. The ways in which those persons inteviewed experienced Health and Well-being as a form of Power varied from security in significant interpersonal relations (I_{11}, I_{12}, I_{21}, I_{27}) to a feeling of control over one's own political fate (I_{15}, I_{27}). In certain cases, this feeling was more diffuse and passive, and was expressed as hope (I_{17}, I_{19}, I_{28}). Hélène and Jean Dupont, for example, did not feel that their own active participation was essential to the Parti Québécois. It was as though they expected to be saved by faith alone; what mattered most to them was that they got from the movement a truth that would in itself set them free. Voting for PQ candidates, and even participation in discussion groups was for them more a profession of faith in that truth than a source of strength for the Party. The boys in the pool (I_{28}) also conveyed a feeling of hope for the future, although their precise relationship to the movement could not be ascertained.

The way in which Separatism contributed to these individuals' Health and Well-being was primarily as a particular type of Power—one is tempted to call it an "enlightened power," since there is a strong element of this value in it—and also as a particular form of enlightenment that had strong ideological overtones. All three of those who experienced Well-being primarily in the form of Enlightenment (I_{18}, I_{20}, I_{23}) had been able to resolve long-standing conflicts, which had provoked anxiety, by joining the PQ. Martin Blain could not have expressed it better when he said that Separatism had validated his values. In addition, Separatism offered relief of anxiety by presenting a path of informed political action to a more or less defined future.

It is not surprising that in two cases (I_{25}, I_{28}) Health and Well-being was experienced in terms of Respect. The pride, the satisfaction with the future as predicted by the Separatist movement, was evident in the responses of the two twelve-year-old swimmers. They appeared to have been spared the "lesson" of Papineau; they found the present and future Quebec interesting and exciting. For Paul Martin, whose self-esteem had fluctuated for years, Separatism had brought a new kind of security, based on self-acceptance and a new independence from the unsympathetic opinions of other Canadians that had been part of his self-reflected appraisal.

It is interesting that only two of the persons interviewed (I_7, I_{12}) identified Affection as the most important element in their sense of Well-being. For them, Affection might be interpreted, if not as Power, then as a certain security that was most directly experienced in interpersonal relations. Both Sebastian Dupré and Jacques Roche could be classified as intellectuals, men whose training and present occupation provided the opportunity for reflection on their own values. It appeared that the emotional support that Sebastian got from other young people provided a social core within which he faced no hostility and where he could find sufficiently satisfying relationships to offset the difficulties of the tasks he had set for himself on the outside. This small area where he no longer felt powerless in interpersonal relationships was thus an extremely important resource for his contributions to the Separatist movement. For Jacques Roche, Separatism had brought a similar benefit, although it is doubtful that this security played quite so crucial a role in his commitment to the movement or to the PQ. His commitment was essentially an intellectual one; the satisfaction and security that he experienced as a result of the "collective dimension" enhanced his pleasure in life and in those relationships which were important to him.

NOTES

1. Harry Stack Sullivan, *The Fusion of Psychiatry and Social Science* (New York: Norton, 1964), p. 250.

2. Harry Stack Sullivan, Sullivan, *The Interpersonal Theory of Psychiatry* (New York: Norton, 1953), p. 22, as quoted by John M. Lincourt and Paul V. Olczak, "C. S. Peirce and H. S. Sullivan on the Human Self," *Psychiatry. Journal for the Study of Interpersonal Processes* 37 (1974):80.

14 • Summary

In this part, the values Power, Wealth, Respect, Enlightenment, Affection, and Health and Well-being have been taken as a given. Although some reference is made to their relative significance in contemporary Quebec, there was no attempt to prestructure these values or to establish empirically a model that would be generally valid for this society. What has been offered here is a description, based on empirical findings, of the way Separatism as an independent variable functions in contemporary Quebec by operationalizing a given set of values.

These values are experienced by the individual as secondary gains, forming a substructure that reinforces the rational elements of political choice. For the French Canadians interviewed, Power, Respect, and Enlightenment were essential functions of the substructure, although each of these values functioned differently. Power and Enlightenment were pivotal: they were mutually facilitative to a very marked degree, and highly facilitative of all the other values as well. Enlightenment was experienced far more intensely than any other value; Power was not experienced intensely, but it did more to promote a general sense of Well-being than any other value. Respect was experienced almost as intensely as Enlightenment. Unlike Enlightenment and Power, however, it was not as highly facilitative of the other values. It was strongly facilitated by Enlightenment; in turn, it tended to facilitate Power.

From these observations it is possible to conclude that Separatism in Quebec supports and sustains itself chiefly through the interaction of these three functions. These functions are values made operative through the movement's appeal to the needs of individuals. Its primary function, then, is the manner in which it satisfies the need for Power; it also satisfies the need for Respect, which again tends to facilitate Power. Its secondary function, then, is the highly complex and diffuse way in which it satisfies the need for Power and ultimately promotes a sense of well-being and satisfaction.

Separatism flourishes because it satisfies those needs created by the circumstances of Quebec's history, needs that, for an increasing number of people, are not met by any other ideology. In part 2, we have seen how Separatism answered these needs in the lives of twelve individuals, and how federalism served this function in the life of a thirteenth. With the accession to power of the Parti Québecois, the Separatist challenge is stronger than ever before. Its ultimate success will depend on whether the ideology of survival and its appeal to a culturally specific value system can be made broad enough to outpace the competing ideology of accommodation.

Part 4
Conclusion

Memory, Enlightenment, and the Colonial Experience

The significance of memory in defining the ideology of the present is well illustrated in the case of Quebec. Without a historical identity, the French Canadian nation and those attitudes intrinsic to belief in independence could not exist. Yet it is important to remember that memory itself is constantly being redefined in the light of present conventions and experience. At the individual as well as collective level, memory "can be understood only as a capacity for the organization and reconstruction of past experiences and impressions in the service of present needs, fears and interests."[1] This interaction of past and present experience, of memory and understanding, makes Enlightenment the central function of Separatism. The perception of grievances and needs, and the assurance that these are being met, are aspects of the Enlightenment function *(fE)* of Separatism.

But once we accept the premise that memory and experience are mutually facilitative, we are compelled to ask, Under what conditions are those patterns of needs and values which Separatism satisfies most likely to arise? When do people *need* to remember?

The role of memory is perhaps most influential in Northern Ireland, where the Catholic minority has sought to liberate itself from British rule for nearly a century.[2] There, as in Quebec, the state-of-siege mentality has recorded centuries-old defeats at the hands of English conquerors. A team of English sociologists, observing the present conflict situation, noted that "an awareness of Cromwell's massacres at Drogheda and Wexford and of the decisive Protestant victory at the Boyne is socialized into school children and it becomes as much a part of the consciousness of belonging to each faith as being Black is for an American Negro."[3] In all three cases, memory serves as a focus for group identification and inter-group differentiation.

The introduction of a political myth appears to follow the breakdown of traditional social structures as if entering a vacuum created by their collapse. Here memory serves to construct and reinforce a set of demands to be implemented in the future, supplanting or superseding the traditional structures no longer available. Such is the case in Quebec, where the resurgence of Separatism follows a period of unprecedented economic integration and profound social change. In Northern Ireland, the 1960s witnessed a similar coincidence, with the Catholic minority's demands for union with the Republic of Ireland (and the severing of constitutional ties with Great Britain) following the expansion of English economic influence, the weakening of the traditional Protestant elite, and the movement of Catholics into the middle class. In both cases, demands for social and political reform were played out against a background of historical antagonisms. These demands wrought such significant changes in the prevailing social structures that a meaningful future could best be defined by reference to the past, as reconstructed in the light of the present. In both cases, the present conflict situation appears to determine just how the past will be remembered. Thus, many French Canadian Separatists view the Act of Confederation as having been motivated chiefly by a desire for economic exploitation; this lends credence to the argument that present economic difficulties can be ascribed to the constitutional structure, but can be resolved through independence. Similarly, Bernadette Devlin recalls that "at the [Protestant] state school they teach that the Act of Union was brought about to help strengthen the trade agreements between England and Ireland. We were taught that it was a malicious attempt to bleed Ireland dry of her linen industry which was affecting English cotton."[4] Austria-Hungary appears to provide another instance where the interaction of past and present experience served to convince a significant portion of the population that their needs could not be met so long as they remained in the empire. In the case of Austria-Hungary, the "distinct historical consciousness" of each of the twenty-two nations that made up the Empire, and the feeling of "being foreign," which had endured for nearly 400 years, were important factors in the rejection of Franz Joseph's attempts at economic integration as exploitative, and ultimately in the breakup of the empire. A similar situation exists in Cyprus, where Greek demands for Enosis, or union with Greece, incorporate memories of the Hellenistic age, reinterpreted in terms of the present ethnic conflict, in the political myth. The vitality of nationalist movements such as these may be ascribed, at least in part, to the intensity of present perceived needs, fears and interests, and the corresponding intensity with which the past must then be recalled. The success of each movement in articulating an appropriate political myth is of course a variable. Nevertheless, it can be stated that in situations of intense intergroup conflict, nationalist and separatist movements are most likely to sustain themselves through their Enlightenment function. When conflict is intense, when life is uncertain, people need to remember the histories that encourage and identify them.

The conditions that give rise to ethnic conflict and ultimately precipitate nationalist and separatist movements appear to be less related to political or economic than to intellectual factors. It is almost axiomatic that, given the choice, individuals will identify with a political system that meets their perceived needs and values. It is far less important that their real political and economic needs be met than that their perceived needs be satisfied, and it is this ability to structure the perceived needs of a given society that gives movements such as French Canadian Separatism their political vitality.

The experience of other bi- and multi-ethnic states serves to illustrate this point. One of the most divisive issues in any bi- or multi-ethnic state has been the language issue. While the language issue does involve very real political and economic needs, it is also highly symbolic of other needs, especially Respect and Well-being. Success in dealing with this issue—which is one of the bases for ethnic identification—does much to convince potential dissidents that the needs of their ethnic group are being met.

Thus, the Belgian experience represents an effort to deal with problems of ethnic identification through an attempt to solve the language issue before a serious separatist challenge develops. As in Canada, pressure for decentralization has traditionally come from the less-affluent, less-influential ethnic minority. One significant difference should be noted here, however: Flemish, the language spoken by a majority of the population, has a distinctly inferior status—that is, it tends to be confined to one national group, while French, the language of the minority is widely learned and spoken. Thus, the Walloon minority are not confronted with the same dilemma of ethnic identity versus social and economic mobility as are their French Canadian counterparts. Nevertheless, in the period after World War II conflict between the two ethnic groups became so intense that an attempt was made to solve it by political means, through the creation of a linguistic border in 1962–63. The result is that Belgium now functions as a bilingual, quasi-federal system, a solution that appears to satisfy both groups.

In Switzerland ethnic and linguistic identifications were successfully integrated with a Swiss identity by means of a federal constitution, which combined cantonal control over language policy with the right of every Swiss citizen to address his government in his own language, or more precisely, in one of the three official languages.[5] According to Friedrich, the "habit of equal treatment for all Swiss, regardless of their nationality . . . has served to build a powerful civic pride in Switzerland."[6] The success of this constitutional attempt at dealing with language policy symbolizes the capability of the federal system to deliver benefits that might not otherwise be enjoyed, and thus tends to minimize frustration and promote an almost universal feeling that the present system is beneficial. Yet it must be emphasized that Swiss unity is based more on belief in federalism than on the federal system itself. One Swiss political scientist has attributed the success of this federal system to the balance between individualism and faith in the federal ideal; this has served as an "antidote to divisive forces and avoided serious conflict."[7] Underlying and serving this faith are the legend of William Tell and the memory of centuries of defending Switzerland's borders against the expansionist efforts of her neighbors.[8]

From the experience of Switzerland and Belgium in coping with the divisive forces of ethnic identification, it is possible to conclude that national identification represents an option for whichever level of political organization will deliver the benefits the individual has been conditioned to expect. Those who believe their needs can be met only by Quebec will opt for Separatism, while those who believe these needs can best be served by the present structure (or by a modification of the present structure) will consider themselves Canadians and choose federalism. In the case of Switzerland and Belgium, no serious Separatist movement has developed because most people are convinced that their needs are best served by the present arrangements. They thus tend to identify themselves as Swiss or Belgian, without conflict with their cantonal or provincial affiliations as Vaudois or Walloon.

The success that both countries have had in dealing directly with the language issue gives some indication of the role played by linguistic factors in directing and symbolizing national identification.

The fact that a given ethnic group speaks French (or Flemish or German) may well provide the necessary focus for a nationalist movement. In Canada, speaking French has both a symbolic meaning, in that it links one to a distinct historical experience and to the specific consciousness that attaches to it, and a social reality, in that it usually limits the opportunities available to the individual within Canadian society. The policy of bilingualism represents an effort by the federal government to deal with this social reality by improving the status of the French language throughout Canada; however, in 1974 the Quebec Legislature took a step in a different direction by instituting French as the official language of the Province. The policy of *unilinguisme*, or monolingualism, as it is called in English, represents an attempt by the Liberal government of Quebec to diminish the appeal of Separatism by dealing directly with the symbolic and social issues. It may be viewed as one attempt to serve the functions of Separatism by political means.

By contrast, Ottawa's inability to deal swiftly and effectively with the language issue has served to convince many French Canadians that the present system of government is incapable of meeting their overall needs.

The Austro-Hungarian empire provides an example of a situation where failure to recognize the perceived needs of ethnic minorities led ultimately to the disintegration of the state. Here, the failure of the *Ausgleich* of 1867 to forge a stable multi-ethnic state even after 400 years of common experience has been attributed to the lack of attitudes favoring unity. According to Jaszy, "All the nations lived as moral and intellectual strangers to one another." Civic education might have promoted unity and countered the various separatist ideas and irredentist propaganda current at the time, but there was none. The ethnic minorities thus had no cause to believe that their needs could be met within the structure of the empire, and the flaws of this political instrument combined with economic and social grievances to convince them that dissolution was their only recourse.

The experiences of Austria-Hungary, Switzerland, and Belgium indicate that political solutions are successful only when reinforced by attitudes favorable to the preservation of the bi-ethnic system. In Belgium, the political solution has been less successful because it is only partially satisfactory to the French-speaking minority, who prefer more decentralization.

The success of some bi-ethnic states in finding acceptable solutions seems to be premised in the end upon whether a colonial suppression once existed. How this can be combatted by integrationists is scarcely known.

The ideology of the conquered nation presents perhaps the greatest obstacle to the survival of multi-ethnic states, and the experience of Austria-Hungary may well be repeated in Quebec, if the Parti Québécois continues to increase its appeal. The most successful challenge to Separatism would be the introduction of a new ideology, capable of accommodating and superseding it, and sufficient economic and social change to support its appeal. If a majority of Quebecers continue to believe that their needs and values are best satisfied by remaining in confederation, the ideological and political challenge of Separatism may dissipate. If, however, no competing ideology is successful in defeating Separatism, it appears likely that the federal structure of Canada will ultimately be replaced by a new kind of association, one mutually agreed upon by two sovereign nations. No longer a conquered group, many former Separatists may then one day find themselves embracing a new ideology of coexistence.

NOTES

1. Ernest G. Schachtel, *Metamorphosis* (New York: Basic Books, 1959), p. 284.

2. The political efforts that culminated in the Government of Ireland Acts of 1914 and 1920 and the Anglo Irish Treaty of 1921 may be traced to the Home Rule debates that began in 1880.

3. R. S. P. Elliott and John Hickie, *Ulster: A Case Study in Conflict Theory* (London: Longmans, 1971), p. 32.

4. Bernadette Devlin, *The Price of My Soul* (London: Pan Books, 1971), p. 62.

5. Kenneth C. Wheare, *Federal Government* (London: Oxford University Press, 3rd Ed., 1953), p. 45.

6. Carl J. Friedrich, *Trends of Federalism in Theory and Practice* (New York: Praeger, 1968), p. 150.

7. G. A. Chevalluz, *La Suisse ou le sommeil du juste* (Lausanne: Payot, 1967), p. 140.

8. Georg Thürer, *Free and Swiss* (London: Oswald Wolff, 1970), pp. 20–22.

A Note on the Methodology

In examining the way Separatism operates, the need to distinguish between those circumstances which give rise to an ideological response and those which support and sustain it become apparent. Despite the richness of the source material, most analyses of Separatism were historical, with many exhibiting a clearly historicist bias.[1] The result of this method was a heavy emphasis on macropolitical, historical, mass conditions, and virtually none on micropolitical, current individual response. All too often the focus was not on Separatism itself, but upon its preconditions.

The critical significance of Separatism as a current, developing phenomenon—not only in Quebec, but throughout the world—made the inadequacy of the literature all the more frustrating. It appeared that the problem was due in part to the lack of any methodology for studying the *current* basis of an ideological movement. The question that seemed most important was the one never asked: How does Separatism work? Because of the contemporary relevance of Separatism and the failure of most writers to tackle this most important issue, it seemed that a functional analysis would be most appropriate. In order to do this, however, a suitable method would have to be found.

It seemed best to begin with a working distinction between the historical and functional aspects of Separatism. These categories overlap at points, but they make it possible to identify what Separatism *does* by distinguishing it from what causes it. The next step was to refine and clarify this working definition of function. The question "How does Separatism work?" was rephrased as "What does Separatism do?" or "What are the things that Separatism can do?" The need for a workable, researchable definition was an important consideration here. The lack of empirical studies or of sufficient data to answer these questions meant that it would be necessary to design an original questionnaire to gather the necessary information. The anticipated limitations of the interview situation were thus a most significant factor in the selection of a research strategy. Since the primary reference would be the individual respondents themselves, it seemed most appropriate to begin with their responses. These would indicate just how Separatism was important to each of them, and, given the right questions, what benefits it offered them (or, more specifically, what benefits the respondents thought it offered). For these individual respondents, then, the perceived gains could be considered functions of Separatism.

In designing the questionnaire, the most important task was to find a structure that could be used to elicit all of the ways in which Separatism could be beneficial (or detrimental, as the case might be) to any individual. The broadest possible structure was therefore sought. Lasswell and Kaplan's eightfold classification of values offered one possibility, but certain categories were not readily distinguishable from one another.[2] For this reason, de Grazia's sixfold classification was used. The values Power, Wealth, Respect (including Self-respect), Enlightenment, Affection (including Loyalty), and Health and Well-being had the advantage of being readily comprehended by the respondent, and the lesser number of categories made for a shorter interview.

The questionnaire covered four types of information—personal data, attitudes toward Separatism in Quebec, functions of Separatism, and the nature of political participation.

ATTITUDES FOR OR AGAINST SEPARATISM IN QUEBEC

    1.0. Interview #
    2.0. Age _____ under 25 (specify) _____
                  _____ 25–38
                  _____ 39–50
                  _____ 51–65
                  _____ 65 or over
    3.0 Occupation
    4.0. In your opinion, what is the extent of the separatist movement today?
    4.1. Has it undergone significant change during the last 10–12 years?
    4.2. What change do you expect to see in the next 5 years?
    5.0. Do you think Quebec will one day become independent?
    5.1. To what degree independent?
    5.2. How will this come about?
    5.3. How do you feel about this?

6.0. What impact does Separatism have on the average French Canadian, inside or outside Quebec, today?

6.1. What impact has it had on you personally—has it been good, bad, or a "mixed blessing"?

7.0. Has Separatism had a positive or negative effect on you in *economic* terms?

7.1. Does it affect your occupation or income, either positively or negatively?

7.2. Can you think of any other way in which it affects you economically?

7.3. Would you gain more, in *current, economic* terms, from supporting Separatism or Federalism?

7.4. Why?

8.0. Has Separatism had a positive or negative effect on you in terms of political power?

8.1. Does the existence of Separatism give you more power, personally?

8.2. Does the existence of Separatism give more power to any group or organization of which you are a member?

8.3. Does the existence of Separatism give more power to any group or organization of which you are *not* a member, but which you generally agree with?

8.4. Does the existence of Separatism give you *less* power, directly or indirectly?

8.5. Would you gain more, in terms of *actual power* now, from supporting Separatism or Federalism?

8.6. Would this power diminish if there were no such thing as Separatism?

9.0. Has Separatism brought greater respect to the average French Canadian?

9.1. Which French Canadians are *more* respected now, as a result of Separatism?

9.2. Who respects them?

9.3. Does the average French Canadian have more or less self-respect as a result of Separatism?

9.4. Which French Canadians are *less* respected now, as a result of Separatism?

9.5. Who respects them less?

9.6. Would you gain more respect, in *current* terms, from supporting Separatism or federalism?

9.7. Why?

10.0. Much has been said about the raising of class consciousness, national consciousness, and the like. Has the average French Canadian's feelings about his history and culture changed as a result of Separatism?

10.1. Is the average French Canadian better *informed* as a result of Separatism?

10.2. Are you personally better informed as a result?

10.3. Is the average French Canadian better *educated*, formally, as a result of Separatism?

10.4. Are you better educated, as a result?

10.5. Would you be better educated and/or informed, as a result of supporting Separatism or Federalism?

10.6. Why?

11.0. Have you experienced any greater loyalty or affection from anyone as a result of the existence of Separatism?

11.1. Would you gain more, in terms of loyalty and/or affection, from supporting Separatism or Federalism?

11.2. From whom?

11.3. Why?

12.0. How have your health and well-being been affected by the existence of Separatism?

12.1. Would your *present* health and/or well-being (or sense of well-being) be better as a result of supporting Separatism or Federalism?

12.2. Why?

13.0. How would you describe a Separatist?

13.1. What would you characterize as separatist attitudes?

14.0. How would you describe a federalist?

14.1. What would you characterize as federalist attitudes?

15.0. Is there a Separatist ideology?

16.0. Would you consider yourself a Separatist or a federalist?

16.1. Why?

17.0. In what ways do you support either Separatism or federalism? Please list as many as apply under each category.

Membership in political organizations:

Membership in other organizations:

Discussion groups:

Discussion informally:

Discussion within the family. Do you try to persuade anyone?

Meetings:

Church affiliation:

Public speaking:

Writing:

Distributing information:

Reading:

(Which newspapers do you read regularly?)

(Among those authors who have written on the subject, which have you read?)

Have you held any official position in the government, federal, provincial, or local?

Have you carried out any minor function, such as poll-watching, registering voters, and the like?

Have you made any financial contribution to any political organization? Has any organization which you belong to contributed to any political organization?

Is there any other way in which you are supporting either Separatism or federalism, in *economic* terms?

Other:

Not all of the respondents answered every question, although they were given the opportunity to do so. However, this did not present any significant obstacle to the collection and interpretation of data. Due to the informal nature of the interview, questions not answered directly were usually answered indirectly. Where no answer was given, an inference could usually be made on the basis of the context and material. In one or two instances, the respondent's perception of a specific benefit conflicted with the interviewer's.[3] In such cases, an interpreted response was entered, and used in the tabulation. Any such occurrences are noted in the case reports and in the analysis that follows. In those cases where no response or inference was possible, "n.a." is used to indicate that the data was not available.

The nature of the interview and its administration dictated a small sample. Given the limited financial resources available for this study, no attempt was made to assemble a representative sample. The respondents represent themselves. However, an effort was made to interview people from as many walks of life as possible, in an attempt to elicit as broad a spectrum of opinion as possible. The range of occupations included workers as well as professors. The choice of respondents was limited by an extreme reluctance on the part of most Quebecers to discuss their intimate political opinions with a stranger, particularly an *Anglophone*. Approximately half of those who did respond to the questionnaire agreed to do so because of some mutual acquaintance or similar circumstance.

The interviews were conducted in New York, Montreal, Quebec City, and rural areas of Quebec in the period from June 20 to August 31, 1973. The questionnaire was used in 20 of them; some other interviews produced tabulable results which are incorporated with them. Since it was later decided to restrict the analysis to *Francophones*, it became necessary to discard one of the interviews based on the questionnaire and all but four of the others.[4] The tabulations that appear in part 2 are the result of a total of 23 interviews and conversations, 14 with persons who believed in Separatism (and are therefore loosely classified as Separatists) and 9 with individuals who chose federalism (and are thus classified as federalists). Eleven of these encounters are described in the case reports that constitute part 2, and an attempt is made therein to describe the circumstances and special characteristics of the interviews. One thing was consistent throughout: the broad categories and simple language of the questionnaire made the questions easy to grasp. There was thus little difficulty with interpretation, and redefinition of the questions was not usually necessary. In some cases the respondents preferred to answer in English. This was permitted only where the use of the second language did not inhibit the respondent's emotional response, freedom of association, or vocabulary. If this type of inhibition became apparent in the course of the interview, French was substituted. In the three cases where this became necessary the respondent preferred to have the questions asked in English, but answered in French.

The wealth and richness of the data accumulated made it necessary to limit the scope and emphasis of this analysis to the functions of Separatism for the individuals who responded to the questionnaire.

The strategy for analyzing these functions was defined only after the data was collected. In the course of writing the case reports it become fairly obvious that the intensity of each function for each individual could be indicated on a 1 to 5 scale, and that the results could be tabulated. It was also apparent that the *mode*, or the way in which each of these values affected the individual, could be identified. However, these results seemed curiously unsatisfactory. For one thing, they appeared strangely unidimensional. One very basic impression, which could not be served by the tabulation of the discrete functions, was the degree to which each individual's values functioned as an integrated system. It seemed that the dynamic aspect of these individuals' collective response to Separatism lay in the relations among these functions.

Lasswell and Kaplan's concept of *facilitation* offered one means of empirically relating the various functions of Separatism. *Facilitation* is defined as "support among acts. . . . Acts are facilitated when each aids the progress to completion of the others."[5] By extending this notion to include sentiments as well as acts, it was possible to integrate all of the functions of Separatism. For example, the increased self-respect that an individual experienced as a result of Separatism could be identified in certain cases as the function *most* facilitating an individual's ability to get a good job and gain economically. Hence, the function Respect would be identified as facilitating Wealth. In this analysis, six charts were prepared, one for each function of Separatism. Respondents were listed individually, and the intensity of the function was entered for each individual. In addition, the *one* other function that most facilitated the enjoyment or experience of that function was noted. In some cases, this was clearly indicated by the respondent; in others, interpretation was necessary. The tapes, completed questionnaires, and case reports were carefully consulted in the preparation of these charts.

The concept of facilitative relations among functions has apparently not been utilized in any previous study. Its application here is admittedly experimental, and the success of the present attempt can be assessed only if future research strategies utilize this technique. At present, the value of this approach may be seen in its capacity to functionally relate the elements of an individual's response to political phenomena and to transpose the resultant patterns of individual response to a collective level. In this way it is possible to learn how Separatism operates and to discover why the "collective myth," as articulated by the present movement, plays such an important role in Quebec's politics.

NOTES

1. Most of the material on Separatism falls into one or more of the following classifications: explanation (which may be historical or sociological), polemic (either Separatist or Federalist), and legal (which encompasses both analysis and recommendations).

2. Harold D. Lasswell and Abraham Kaplan, *Power and Society: A Framework for Political Inquiry* (New Haven: Yale University Press, 1965). The categories Skill and Enlightenment and Respect and Rectitude were condensed in this analysis into Enlightenment and Respect.

3. This occurred primarily in the case of Power. The two revolutionaries, for example, denied that they had experienced any increase in power, although it was clear that they had. Similarly, Sebastian Dupré (Interview 7) believed he had no power, whereas actually he had acquired the type that was most meaningful to him. This attitude appears to reflect the survival of traditional, 19th-century attitudes toward political power.

4. Anglophones and immigrants who speak a language other than French tend almost exclusively toward federalism. Their reasons for choosing federalism are obviously different from those of *Franchophones*, and it can be argued that since the option of Separatism is not addressed to them, it is not really an *available* option, and they do not actually have a choice.

5. Lasswell and Kaplan, *Power and Society*, p. 19.

Bibliography

Aiyar, S. P. *Federalism and Social Change*. New York: Asia Publishing House, 1961.

d'Allemagne, André. *Le RIN et les débuts du mouvement indépendantist québécois*. Montreal: Editions de l'Etincelle, 1974.

Almond, Gabriel A., and Sidney Verba. *The Civic Culture: Political Attitudes and Democracy in Five Nations*. Princeton, N.J.: Princeton University Press, 1963.

Apter, David E. *Ideology and Discontent*. New York: The Free Press, 1964.

————. *Political Change*. London: Frank Cass, 1973.

Barbeau, Raymond. *La Libération économique du Québec*. Montreal: Les Editions de l'Homme, 1963.

Benjamin, Jacques. "La Minorité en état bicommunitaire: quatre études de cas." *Canadian Journal of Political Science* 4 (1970): 477–96.

Bergeron, Gerard, *Du duplessisme au johnsonisme, 1956–1966*. Montreal: Editions Parti Pris, 1967.

Bergeron, Leandre. *The History of Quebec: A "Patriote's" Handbook*. Toronto: NC Press, Ltd., 1971.

Bernard, André. *Quebec: Elections 1976*. Montreal: Hurtubise, HMH, 1976.

————. *What Does Quebec Want?* Toronto: James Lorimer and Company, 1978.

Boily, Robert. *La Réforme Electorale au Québec*. Montreal: Les Editions du Jour, 1971.

Bonjour, E., H. S. Offer, and G. R. Potter. *A Short History of Switzerland*. Oxford: Clarendon Press, 1955.

Boulet, Giles. *Nationalisme et séparatisme*. Trois-Rivières: Editions du Sociéte Pierre-Boucher, 1962.

Bowie, Robert R., and Carl J. Friedrich, eds. *Studies in Federalism*. Boston: Little, Brown, 1954.

Brady, Alexander. *Democracy in the Dominions: A Comparative Study of Institutions*, 3d edition. Toronto: University of Toronto Press, 1962.

Brunet, Michel. *Canadians et Canadiens.* Montreal: Editions Fides, 1955.

———. *La présence anglaise et les Canadiens.* Montreal: Librairie Beauchemin, 1958.

———. "Trois dominates de la pensée canadienne-française: l'agriculturalisme, l'anti-étatisme, et le messianisme." *Ecrits du Canada Français,* 3 (1957): 31–117.

Cameron, David. *Nationalism, Self-determination and the Quebec Question.* Toronto: Macmillan of Canada (Canadian Controversies Series), 1974.

Campbell, D. T., and R. A. Levine, "A proposal for cooperative cross-cultural research on ethnocentrism." *Journal of Conflict Resolution* 5 (1961): 82–108.

Canada, Royal Commission of Bilingualism and Biculturalism. *Final Report.* 4 vols. (A. Davidson Dunton, André Laurendeau, Co-chairmen). Ottawa: Queen's Printer, 1968–1970.

Chaput, Marcel. *Why I Am a Separatist.* Translated by Robert A. Taylor. Toronto: Ryerson Press, 1961.

Chaput-Rolland, Solange. *My Country, Canada or Quebec?* Toronto: Macmillan of Canada, 1966.

———. *Reflections: Quebec Year One.* Montreal: Chateau Books, Ltd., 1968.

Chevalluz, G. A. *La Suisse ou le sommeil du juste.* Lausanne: Payot, 1967.

Chodos, Robert, and Nick Auf der Mar, eds. *Quebec: A Chronicle 1968–1972.* Toronto: James Lorimer and Co., 1972.

Clark, S. D. *Movements of Political Protest in Canada, 1640–1840.* Toronto: University of Toronto Press, 1959.

Codding, George A. *The Federal Government of Switzerland.* Boston: Houghton Mifflin, 1961.

Cohen, M. "Canada and Quebec in North America: A Pattern for Fulfillment." *Queen's Quarterly* 75 (Fall 1968): 389–400.

Constitutionalism and Nationalism in Lower Canada. Essays by Fernand Ouellet, Laurence A. H. Smith, D. G. Creighton, W. H. Parker. Introduction by Ramsay Cook. Toronto: University of Toronto Press, 1969.

Cook, Ramsay. *Canada and the French Canadian Question.* Toronto: Macmillan of Canada, 1966.

———. *French Canadian Nationalism: An Anthology.* Toronto: Macmillan of Canada, 1969.

Corbett, Edward M. *Quebec Confronts Canada.* Baltimore: Johns Hopkins Press, 1967.

Crepeau, P. A., and C. B. MacPherson. *The Future of Canadian Federalism.* Toronto: University of Toronto Press, 1965.

Dahl, Robert A., *Political Oppositions in Western Democracies*. New Haven, Conn.: Yale University Press, 1966.

Dawson, Richard E., and Kenneth Prewitt. *Political Socialization*. Boston: Little, Brown (Series in Comparative Politics), 1969.

Debuyst, Frederic. *La Fonction Parlementaire en Belgique: Mecanismes d'access et images*. Brussels: Centre de Recherche et d'information socio-politique (C.R.I.S.P.), 1967.

Desbiens, Jean Paul. *Les insolences du Frère Untel*. Montreal: Les Editions de l'homme, 1960.

Deutsch, Karl W. *Nationalism and Social Communication*. Cambridge: Technology Press of the Massachusetts Institute of Technology, 1953.

Devlin, Bernadette. *The Price of My Soul*. London: Pan Books, 1971.

Le Devoir. *Le Québec dans le Canada de demain*. 2 vols. Montreal: Editions du jour, 1967.

Dew, Edward. "Testing Elite Perceptions of Deprivation and Satisfaction in a Culturally Plural Society." *Comparative Politics* 6 (1974): 271–85.

Dion, Léon. *Nationalismes et politique au Québec*. Montreal: Hurtubise HMH.

———. *Quebec: The Unfinished Revolution*. Montreal: McGill-Queen's University Press, 1976.

Dolment, Marcelle, and Marcel Barthe. *La Femme au Québec*. Montreal: Les Presses libres, 1973.

Dube, Rodolphe. *Cent ans d'injustice? Un beau rêve: le Canada*. Montreal: Editions du jour, 1967.

Duchacek, Ivo D. *Comparative Federalism: The Territorial Dimension of Politics*. New York: Holt, Rinehart and Wilson, 1970.

Duverger, Maurice. *Political Parties*. New York: Science Editions, 1965.

Earle, Valerie, *Federalism: Infinite Variety in Theory and Practice*. Itasca, Ill.: F. E. Peacock, Publishers, 1968.

Eccles, W. J. *France in America*. New York: Harper and Row, 1973.

Edelman, Murray. *The Symbolic Uses of Politics*. Urbana, Ill.: University of Illinois Press, 1964.

Elazar, Daniel J. "Federalism." *International Encyclopedia of the Social Sciences*, 5: 353–67.

Elliot, R. S. P., and John Hickie. *Ulster: A Case Study in Conflict Theory*. London: Longman Group, Ltd., 1971.

Enlow, Cynthia H. *Ethnic Conflict and National Development*. Boston: Little, Brown, 1973.

Fanon, Frantz. *The Wretched of the Earth*. Translated by Constance Farrington. New York: Grove Press, 1966.

Faribault, Marcel. *La Revision Constitutionnelle*. Montreal: Fides, 1970.

————. *Vers une nouvelle constitution*. Montreal: Editions Fides, January 1968.

————, and Robert M. Fowler. *Ten to One*. Toronto: McClelland and Stewart, 1965.

Favreau, Guy. *The Amendment of the Constitution of Canada*. Ottawa: The Queen's Printer, 1965.

Franck, Thomas M., ed. *Why Federations Fail*. New York: New York University Press, 1968.

Friedrich, Carl J. *Europe: An Emergent Nation?* New York: Harper and Row, 1969.

————. "Rights, Liberties, Freedoms: A Reappraisal." *American Political Science Review* 57 (1963): 841–54.

————. *Trends of Federalism in Theory and Practice*. New York: Praeger, 1968.

Gagnon, C. "The Quebec Liberation Struggle." *New Left Review* 64 (November–December 1970) 62–70.

Garigue, Philippe. *Bibliographie du Québec (1955–1965)*. Montreal: Les Presses de l'Université de Montréal, 1967.

————. *Etudes sur le Canada Française*. Montreal: Faculté des sciences sociales, economiques et politiques, 1958.

————. *L'Option politique du Canada française: Une interpretation de la survivance nationale*. Montreal: Les Editions du Levrier, 1963.

————. *La Vie familiale des Canadiens français*. Montreal: Presses de l'Universite de Montreal, 1970.

Gottleib, A. E., ed. *Human Rights, Federalism and Minorities*. Toronto: Canadian Institute of International Affairs, 1970.

Grazia, Alfred de. *Politics for Better or Worse*. Glenview, Ill.: Scott, Foresman and Co., 1973.

Greeley, Andrew M. *Unsecular Man*. New York: Schocken Books, 1972.

Gurr, Ted Robert. *Why Men Rebel*. Princeton, N.J.: Princeton University Press, 1972.

Hagy, J. W. "Quebec Separatists: The First Twelve Years." *Queen's Quarterly* 76 (Summer 1969): 229–38.

————. "René Lévesque and the Quebec Separatists." *Western Political Quarterly* 24, no. 1 (March 1971): 55–58.

Hare, John, ed. *Les Patriotes 1830–1839*. Montreal: Les Editions Libération, 1971.

Hargrove, E. C. "Nationality, Values and Change: Young Elites in French Canada." *Comparative Politics* 2 (April 1970): 473–500.

Hartz, Louis. *The Founding of New Societies.* New York: Harcourt, Brace and World (Harbinger Books), 1964.

Harvey, Jean Charles. *Pouquoi je suis antiséparatiste.* Montreal: Editions de l'homme, 1962.

Hébert, Anne. *Kamouraska.* New York: Crown Publishers, 1973.

Hémon, Louis. *Maria Chapdelaine.* Montreal: Bibliothèque Canadienne-Française, 1970.

Hoffer, Eric. *The True Believer.* New York: Harper and Row, Perennial Library, 1966.

Hughes, Everett C. *French Canada in Transition.* Chicago: The University of Chicago Press, 1967.

Jacobs, Jane. *The Question of Separatism: Quebec and the Struggle over Sovereignty.* New York: Random House, 1980.

Johnson, Daniel. *Egalité ou indépendance.* Montreal: Editions de l'homme, 1966.

Jones, Richard. *Community in Crises, French Canadian Nationalism in Perspective.* Toronto: McClelland and Stewart, 1967.

Jouvenel, Bertrand de. *On Power.* Boston: Beacon Press, 1969.

Joy, Richard J. *Languages in Conflict: The Canadian Experience.* Toronto: McClelland and Stewart, 1972.

Kelly, G. A. "Biculturalism and Party Systems in Belgium and Canada," in J. Montgomery, Editor, *Public Policy.* Cambridge: Harvard University Press, 1967.

Keyserlingk, R. M. "France and Quebec: The Psychological Basis for their Co-Operation." *Queen's Quarterly* 75 (Spring 1968): 21–32.

Kohn, Hans. *The Age of Nationalism: The First Era of Global History.* New York: Harper and Brothers, 1962.

———. *Nationalism and Liberty.* New York: Macmillan, 1956.

Kroeber, A. L., and C. Kluckhohn. *Culture, a Critical Review of Concepts and Definitions.* Cambridge, Mass.: Peabody Museum of Harvard University, 1952.

La Tondre, D. "Anti-séparatisme et méssianisme au Québec depuis 1960." *Canadian Journal of Political Science* 3, no. 4 (December 1970): 559–78.

Lalaude, Gilles. *In Defence of Federalism: The View from Quebec.* Translated by Jo La Pierre. Toronto: McClelland and Stewart, Ltd, 1978.

Lane, Robert E. *Political Thinking and Consciousness.* Chicago: Markham Publishing Company, 1969.

Larocque, André. *Defis au Parti Québecois.* Montreal: Les éditions du jour, 1971.

Lasswell, Harold D., and Abraham Kaplan. *Power and Society: A Framework for Political Inquiry.* New Haven, Conn.: Yale University Press, 1965.

Laurier, Wilfrid. "Trois Discours sur Riel." *XXIV Ecrits du Canada Français,* 1968, pp. 163–257.

Lazure, Jacques. *La Jeunesse du Québec en révolution.* Montreal: Les Presses de l'Université du Québec, 1971.

LeClerc, Felix. *Cent Chansons.* Montreal: Fides, 1970.

Lecault, Albert, and Alfred O. Hero, eds. *Le nationalisme québecois à la croisée des chemins.* Quebec: Centre québecois des relations internationales, 1975.

Lemelin, Roger. *Pierre le Magnifique.* Montreal: Le Cercle du Livre de France, 1971.

Lemieux, Vincent. "Les élections fédérales de 1957 à 1965 au Québec: un réinterpretation." *Canadian Journal of Political Science* 4 (1970): 395–97.

————. *Quatre élections provinciales au Québec, 1956–1966,* Quebec, Les Presses de l'Université Laval, 1969.

Lévesque, Albert. *La nation canadienne française: son existence, ses droits, ses devoirs.* Montreal: A. Lévesque, 1934.

Lévesque, René. *An Option for Quebec.* Toronto: McClelland and Stewart, 1968.

Lévesque-Dubé, Alice. *Il y a soixante ans.* Montreal, 1943.

Lieberson, Stanley. *Language and Ethnic Relations in Canada.* New York: John Wiley and Sons, 1970.

Lijphart, Arend. "Cultural Diversity and Theories of Political Integration." *Canadian Journal of Political Science* 4 (March 1971): 1–14.

Lipset, Seymour Martin. *Revolution and Counter-revolution: Change and Persistence in Social Structures.* (Revised and updated edition. Garden City, N.Y.: Doubleday (Anchor Books), 1970.

McWhinney, Edward. *Federal Constitution-making for a Multinational World.* Leyden: A. W. Sijthoff, 1966.

Masserman, Jules H., Ed. *Psychoanalysis and Social Process.* New York and London: Grune and Stratton, 1961.

Meekison, J. Peter. *Canadian Federalism, Myth or Reality,* 3/e. Toronto: Methuen, 1977.

Milner, S. H., and H. Milner, *The Decolonization of Quebec: An Analysis of Left-Wing Nationalism.* Tononto: McClelland and Stewart, 1973.

Minville, Esdras. *Le Citoyen canadien-français: notes pour servir à l'enseignement du civisme.* Montreal: Fides, 1946.

Monet, Jacques. *The Last Cannon Shot, A Study of French-Canadian Nationalism, 1837–1850.* Toronto: University of Toronto Press, 1969.

Morchain, Janet. *Search for a Nation: French-English Relations in Canada since 1789.* Toronto: University of Toronto Press, 1969.

Moreno, Francisco Jose. *Between Faith and Reason: An Approach to Individual and Social Psychology.* New York: New York University Press, 1977.

Morin, Claude, *Le Combat québécois.* Montreal: Les Editions du Boréal Express, 1973.

———. *Le Pouvoir québécois en négotiation.* Montreal: Les Editions du Boréal Express, 1972.

———. *Quebec versus Ottawa.* Toronto: University of Toronto Press, 1976.

Morin, Edgar. *The Red and the White: Report from a French Village.* New York: Pantheon, 1970.

Morin, Jacques-Yvan. "Situation et perspectives politiques des Canadiens français." *Politique Etrangère* 34 (1969): 265–88.

Morin Wilfred. *L'Indépendance du Québec: Le Québec aux Québécois.* Montreal: Editions Fides, 1943.

Morrison, Donald G., and H. M. Stevenson. "Cultural Pluralism, Modernization and Conflict: An Empirical Analysis of Sources of Political Instability in African Nations." *Canadian Journal of Political Science* 4 (1971): 82–103.

Mullins, Willard A. "On the Concept of Ideology in Political Science." *American Political Science Review* 66 (1972): 498–510.

Murray, Vera. *Le Parti Québécois: de la fondation à la prise du pouvoir.* Montreal: Hurtubise, HMH, 1976.

Murrow, Casey. *Henri Bourassa and French-Canadian Nationalism: Opposition to Empire.* Montreal: Harvest House, 1968.

Myers, Hugh B. *The Quebec Revolution.* Montreal: Harvest House, 1964.

Nevers, Edmond de. *L'Avenir du peuple canadien-français.* Paris: H. Jouve, 1896.

Newman, Peter C. *A Nation Divided: Canada and the Coming of Pierre Trudeau.* New York: Alfred A. Knopf, 1969.

Nish, Cameron. *Quebec in the Duplessis Era, 1935–1959: Dictatorship or Democracy?* Toronto: The Copp Clark Publishing Company, 1970.

O'Brien, Connor Cruise. *States of Ireland.* New York: Vintage Books, 1971.

O'Leary, Dostaler. *Séparatisme, doctrine constructive.* Montreal: Les éditions des jeunesses patriotes, 1937.

Pagnette, Gilbert, and Raymond Lemieux. *A Quand la réform scolaire?* Montreal: Les Editions du Parti Québécois, 1972.

Paré, Gérard. *Au delà du séparatisme: le Canada que j'ai revu.* Montreal: Editions du jour, 1966.

Pellerin, Jean. *Lettre aux Nationalistes québécois.* Montreal: Editions du jour, 1969.

Pelletier, Gérard. *The October Crisis.* Translated by Joyce Marshall. Toronto: McClelland and Stewart, Ltd., 1971.

Pinard, Maurice. *The Rise of a Third Party: A Study in Crisis Politics.* Engelwood Cliffs, N.J.: Prentice-Hall, 1971.

Power, C. G. "Quebec Nationalism in my Time." *Queen's Quarterly* 75 (Spring 1968): 1–20.

La Presse.

Provencher, Jean. *René Lévesque, Portrait of a Québécois.* Translated by David Ellis. Markham, Ontario: Paper Jacks editions, 1977.

Québec, *Report of the Commission on the Position of the French Language and on Language Rights in Québec* (Glendron Report). 3 vols. Montreal: L'Editeur officiel du Québec, 1972–1973.

Québec: The Threat of Separation by the Telegram (Toronto) Canada 70 team, Toronto: McClelland and Stewart, 1969.

Québec, Government of. *What does Québec Want?* Québec: Information and Publicity Office, 1968.

Quebec, University of. *Fédéralisme et nations.* Montreal: Les Presses de l'Université du Québec, 1971.

The Queen v Louis Riel. With an introduction by Desmond Morton. Toronto: University of Toronto Press, 1974.

Quesnel-Ouellet, Louise. "Régionalisation et conscience politique régionale: la communauté urbaine de Québec." *Canadian Journal of Political Science* 4 (1970): 191–205.

Quoi de Neuf, monthly bulletin of Quebec wing of the Liberal Party of Canada.

Regenstreif, P. "Note on the 'Alternation' of French and English Leaders in the Liberal Party of Canada." *Canadian Journal of Political Science* 2 (March 1969): 118–22.

Reilly, Wayne G. "Political Attitudes among Law Students in Quebec." *Canadian Journal of Political Science* 4 (1970): 122–31.

The Report of the Earl of Durham. New York: E. P. Dutton and Co., 1902.

Riel, Louis. *Journal de Prison. XIII Ecrits du Canada Français*, 1962.

Riker, William H. *Federalism, Origin, Operation, Significance.* Boston: Little, Brown and Co., 1964.

Rioux, Marcel. *Quebec in Question.* Translated by James Boake. Toronto: James Lewis and Samuel, 1971.

———— and Yves Martin. eds. *French-Canadian Society.* 2 vols. Toronto: McClelland and Stewart, Ltd., 1964.

———— and Robert Sevigny. *Les Nouveau citoyens: enquête sociologique sur les jeunes du Québec.*

Royal Society of Canada. *Structures sociales du Canada français.* Toronto: University of Toronto Press, 1966.

Rutan, Gerard F. "Two Views of the Concept of Sovereignty: Canadian—Canadien." *Western Political Quarterly* 24(1971): 446–66.

Sabourin, Louis. *Le Système politique du Canada: Institutions fédérales et Québécoises.* Ottawa: Les Editions de l'Université d'Ottawa, 1970.

Saywell, John. *Quebec 70: A Documentary Narrative.* Toronto: University of Toronto Press, 1971.

Schermerhorn, R. A. *Comparative Ethnic Relations.* New York: Random House, 1970.

Schwartz, M. A. *Public Opinion and Canadian Identity.* Berkeley: University of California Press, 1967.

Scott, Frank, and Michael Oliver, editors. *Quebec States her Case: Speeches and Articles from Quebec in the Year of Unrest.* Toronto: Macmillan of Canada, 1964.

Sequin, Maurice. *L'Idée d'indépendance au Québec: genèse et historique.* Trois-Rivières: Les Editions Boréal express, 1968.

Seton-Watson, Hugh. "Unsatisfied Nationalism." *Journal of Contemporary History* 6, no. 1 (1971): 3–14.

Simeon, Richard. *Federal-Provincial Diplomacy: The Making of Recent Policy in*
————. *The Statute of Westminster and Dominion Status,* 5/e. London: Oxford

————. *Must Canada Fail?* Montreal: McGill-Queen's University Press, 1977, 1979.

Sloan, Thomas. *Quebec: The Not So Quiet Revolution.* Toronto: The Ryerson Press, 1965.

Smiley, Donald V. "The Two Themes of Canadian Federalism." *Canadian Journal of Economics and Political Science* 31(1965): 80–97.

Smith, Bernard. *Le coup d'état du 29 avril.* Montreal: Editions Actualité, 1970.

Spry, G. "Canada: Notes on Two Ideas of Nation in Confrontation." *Journal of Contemporary History,* 6, no. 1 (1971): 173–96.

Sullivan, Harry Stack. *The Fusion of Psychiatry and Social Science.* New York: Norton, 1964.

Thomson, Dale C., ed. *Quebec Society and Politics: Views from the Inside.* Toronto: McClelland and Stewart, 1973.

Tonnies, Ferdinand. *Community and Society*. New York: Harper and Row, 1963.

Tournon, Jean. "Le pluralisme: une mise à mort ratée." *Canadian Journal of Political Science* 4 (1970): 265–79.

Tremblay, Rodrigue. *Indépendance et marché commun Québec–Etats-Unis*. Montreal: Les Éditions du Jour, 1970.

Trudeau, Pierre Elliott. *Federalism and the French Canadians*. New York: St. Martin's Press, 1968.

Vadeboncoeur, Pierre. *La dernière heure et la première, Essai*. Montreal: Les Editions de l'Hexagone, Les Edns. Parti Pris, 1970.

Vahier, Georges. *Essai sur la mentalité canadienne-française*. Paris: H. Champion, 1928.

Vaillancourt, Emile. *Knifed and Thrown Away Like a Dead Cat*. Montreal: 1938.

Vallieres, Pierre. *L'Urgence de choisir*. Montreal: Parti Pris, 1971.

―――. *White Niggers of America*. Translated by Joan Pinkham. Toronto: McClelland and Stewart, 1971.

Van Loon, Richard, and Michael Whittington. *The Canadian Political System, Environment, Structure and Process*. Toronto: McGraw-Hill Co. of Canada, Ltd., 1971.

Vaughan, Frederick, and Patrick and Dwivedi Kyba. *Contemporary Issues in Canadian Politics*. Scarborough (Ontario): Prentice-Hall, 1970.

Wade, Mason, editor. *Canadian Dualism*. Toronto: University of Toronto Press, 1960.

―――. *The French Canadians, 1976–1967*. 2 vols. Toronto: Macmillan of Canada, 1968.

――― ed. *Regionalism in the Canadian Community 1867–1967*. Toronto: University of Toronto Press, 1969.

Waite, P. B. *Canada 1874–1896: Arduous Destiny*. Toronto: McClelland and Stewart, Ltd., 1971.

Weber, Max. *The Theory of Social and Economic Organization*. Translated by A. M. Henderson and Talcott Parsons. Glencoe, Ill.: The Free Press of Glencoe, 1947.

Weil, Gordon L. *The Benelux Nations: The Politics or Small-Country Democracies*. New York: Holt, Rinehart and Winston, 1970.

Wheare, Kenneth C. *Federal Government*. London: Oxford University Press, 1953.

―――. *The Statue of Westminster and Dominion Status*, 5/e. London: Oxford University Press, 1953.

Williams, Robin M., Jr. *The Reduction of Intergroup Tensions.* New York: Social Science Research Council, 1947.

Wood, John R. "Secession—A Comparative Analytical Framework." *Canadian Journal of Political Science* 14:107–34 (1981).

Zoltvany, Yves F., ed. *The French Tradition in America.* Harper and Row, 1969.

————. *The Government of New France: Royal, Clerical or Class Rule?* Scarboro (Ontario): Prentice-Hall of Canada, 1971.

Index